UNDAUNTED

by Graham Reeves

The Story of Bromley in the Second World War

*"Bromley can hold its chin right out and
has the right to look anyone in the face, undaunted.
That is why I am always so glad
to come to the town."*

Admiral Sir Edward Evans, April 1944

FIRST PUBLISHED 1990

ISBN 0 901002 10 0

Printed in Great Britain for Bromley Leisure Services,
Central Library, High Street, Bromley. BR1 1EX

Designed & Printed by The Marketing Portfolio.

*Front cover concept by Maria McCullough,
Bromley Leisure Services*

FOREWORD

I am delighted to have had an opportunity to read this work by local headmaster Graham Reeves.

The second World War touched all our lives in one way or another and, whilst countless books have been written on the subject, this one is particularly valuable because it relates to our own locality: the London Borough of Bromley.

As an avid *Just William* reader when young, and for many years having lived near Oakley Road, the home of Richmal Crompton, I have long believed that the stories were set in that area. The stream in the wood where the Outlaws played was the Ravensbourne in Barnet Wood and the 'Big' houses were The Cedars and Hollydale, alas now gone. The church was Holy Trinity and the fields and farm were Oakley House. I was therefore delighted to read a, to me, William story with real names for his 'home' setting.

The whole work comes alive as it dovetails statistics of war with personal stories of local residents; and I am sure that not only those of you who lived through the period will find it enthralling but also the William Browns and the Violet Elizabeths of today, as they read of how war affected their town in their Borough.

I congratulate the author on his work.

Councillor R.L. Ainsby

Mayor 1989 - 1990

CONTENTS

For Rachel and Eleanor

"For peace comes dropping slow"

W.B. Yeats
'The Lake Isle of Innisfree'

PREFACE

Today we are used to seeing reports of wars and disasters appearing in our newspapers and - with dramatic images - on our television screens. Yet in the comfort of our own homes it is often difficult or even impossible to imagine what it is like to be involved. We still tend to think that such things can never happen to us - and, thankfully, they rarely do.

For those of us who did not actually live through the Second World War it is particularly difficult to have any sort of idea of what it was really like - even more so when our images have been formed by heroic and sanitised books, films and comics and by toy soldiers and other games.
In researching and writing this book I think I have come to a better understanding of other people's experiences.

I hope that, without any sensationalism or sentimentalisation, I am able to give an accurate account of what happened and to communicate some of the understanding. More than anything else I hope that I am able to contribute something to the cause of peace so that their experiences could never be in vain.

Graham Reeves, Elmers End, April 1989

1

RUMOURS OF WAR 1938-39

"And ye shall hear of wars and rumours of wars:
see that ye be not troubled: for all these things must come to pass,
but the end is not yet."
Matthew 24 verse 6

Events in Europe, and especially in Germany, meant that the threat of war was never far from some people's minds throughout the whole of the 1930s. It was in July 1935 that the British government - through the Home Office - issued a circular to County Councils throughout the country, instructing them to make plans for protection against air raids. Kent County Council was slow to act upon the circular, but this did not stop local councils such as Bromley and Beckenham from taking their own action.

Bromley Council set up its Air Raid Precautions Committee in January 1936 with Alderman F. Stafford Clark as Chairman. By October of that year the A.R.P. Committee had received a 22 page report prepared by the Town Clerk, the three principal officers of the Council and the Chief of the Fire Brigade. This report formed the basis of Bromley's plans which were to be developed and put into effect during the following years. At the end of 1936 the Council's Chief Sanitary Officer was sent on a training course at the Civilian Anti-Gas School and on his return was responsible for training others. In March 1938 Lieutenant-Colonel W. Bird started work as full-time A.R.P. Officer for Bromley.

Beckenham's A.R.P. Officer, Lieutenant-Colonel W.J. Howard DSO, was appointed much earlier. He took up his duties in January 1937 and launched the Council's A.R.P. scheme at a public meeting, attended by over a thousand people, in July 1937. An appeal was started for 1,500 volunteers to be trained to do the many tasks that would be needed in the event of war.

In Orpington, the A.R.P. Officer was Colonel K.M. Kirkhope. Speaking at an exhibition in Farnborough Parish Hall at the beginning of March 1938, he told listeners:

"It is your duty to learn how to protect yourselves and how to help your neighbour in the time of an air raid."

The exhibition included gas masks, tin helmets, shovels, buckets, stretchers and rubber-suited models. There was a demonstration of a room which had been set out to defend its occupants against a gas attack, and also a full scale model of a first aid post.

On 14th March, the Home Secretary Sir Samuel Hoare, broadcast a radio appeal for a million volunteers throughout the country. In particular he asked for people to become air raid wardens. He said that they should be men and women who knew and lived in the streets for which they would be responsible. They would make house-to-house calls to advise people how to make their homes safer and to help them try on gas masks. Then, in the event of an air raid, they would patrol the streets and report on the situation to the A.R.P. local headquarters.

Bromley and Orpington now followed Beckenham's example and started recruitment. In Orpington the target was for 3,000 volunteers. Bromley wanted something like 1,800. They were to be trained as air raid wardens, first aid workers, drivers, gas decontamination squads and rescue squads. On top of this there was a need for 250 auxiliary firemen. Over a hundred people volunteered in Bromley within a few days of Sir Samuel Hoare's broadcast, and by the end of the month this figure had risen to 340. The rate slowed down, though, and by the first week of May there had still been only 400 volunteers - a long way short of the number required.

A Government leaflet *What You Can Do* was issued to every home in Bromley together with an appeal for help, but still the response was poor. By August only 120 people had been trained as air raid wardens, compared with the 900 who were needed. This meant that very few gas masks had been given out to local people. In Beckenham, however, there had been 1,200 volunteers for the various A.R.P. duties and over 14,000 masks had already been

issued.
Penge had similar difficulties. By May there were 200 volunteers compared with the 800 needed; and Bertram Varrow, the A.R.P. Officer, said:

"As yet our numbers are nowhere near the total required, and I am anxious to speed things up in that respect. We definitely need more street wardens so that we can get on with the task of fitting out members of the civilian population with their gas masks."

Bromley was divided into seven districts, each with its own A.R.P. Committee. The duties of each Committee were to help with the recruitment of wardens and to arrange meetings for them to instruct members of the public. Yet as Lieutenant- Colonel Bird had pointed out in June:

"Bromley has the instructors, the accommodation and the equipment; only the men and women are missing."

Orpington, in the meantime, appears to have reduced its required number of volunteers from 3,000 to 2,000. Of these 1,500 had to be men because some of the tasks - such as those for decontaminators, rescue men and firemen - were regarded as too strenuous for women. Among the tasks that the 500 women could do was driving the various A.R.P. vehicles. Like Bromley, Orpington was divided into areas - 10 in this case - each with its own head warden.

Not everyone actually supported the plans for protection against air raids. Members of the Peace Pledge Union, for instance, argued that instead of preparing for war the country should be working for peace. There were also objections to the way in which the precautions seemed to be concentrating upon the danger of gas, when many people thought that greater threats were posed by high explosive or incendiary bombs. Answering one such objection from a councillor at a meeting of the Orpington Urban District Council Colonel Kirkhope pointed out that, of all the dangers, gas was the simplest to deal with and therefore all volunteers received that training. He also said:
"The A.R.P. scheme provides for protection of the people against all air risks ... I know that the greatest risks are high explosive bombs,

incendiary bombs and gas bombs. But we cannot protect you against a direct hit. We will, however, protect you against blast and splinters to the best of our ability. Everyone will be instructed as to how to avoid the possibility of fire from incendiary bombs."

By September 1938 the international situation was looking very serious. In March German troops had moved into Austria. Now it looked as if Hitler was intending to invade Czechoslovakia. Monsieur Daladier, the French Prime Minister, said that France would fight to protect Czechoslovakia and expected Britain to do the same. Neville Chamberlain met Hitler for talks in Germany, but when no agreement was reached war looked certain.

During the afternoon of Monday 26th September 1938 local councils throughout the country received from the Home Office telegrams giving instructions to issue gas masks and dig trenches. Suddenly the A.R.P. arrangements were being put into operation for real.

That morning 54,000 gas masks had arrived at Bromley North Station. They were taken by a fleet of lorries to a marquee which had been hurriedly erected in Hayes. The masks were in kit form and had to be put together before they were given out. Three hundred volunteers (including 50 workers who were given time off from their jobs at the Viscose Company) worked all through the Monday night and the next day as well. It was midnight on Tuesday 27th September before all the equipment was ready.

On the morning of Wednesday 28th September 12 lorries and 20 cars collected the gas masks from Hayes and delivered them to 16 halls around Bromley. By six o'clock that evening they were all set out ready for collection.

The halls were open at seven o'clock on Thursday 29th September, but with only a third of the local population having already received masks from the wardens the queues were forming long before that time, and many people had to wait for two hours or more before they were able to get in.

With still only 150 trained wardens to fit the masks and give instructions on their use, it was a very slow process. Yet by midnight on that first day 36,000 had been distributed, and most of the rest

were given out the next evening.
In Beckenham 60 per cent of the population had already received their masks before the emergency was declared, and the wardens already knew the requirements of most of the rest. Tens of thousands of the masks had been delivered to the Town Hall and Hawes Down School on Saturday 24th September. When the Home Office telegram was received at 4.00 p.m. on Monday 26th September, Lieutenant-Colonel Howard immediately contacted three local firms. By 5.00 p.m. one hundred and fifty "factory girls" from Perga Ltd., Frank Burnham, and Twinlocks were working on assembling the gas masks. They were taken by lorries to three regional depots and 15 distribution points; wardens then delivered them by car to people's homes. At the height of the crisis the Town Clerk, C. Eric Stadden, reported to Beckenham Borough Council:

"Despite the apathy of the population, the machinery is working. It was working within an hour of the time that we received notice. At the same time, I should like to say that if there had been an adequate response seventeen months ago, when we first appealed for volunteers, all the fitting would have been done by now."

In Orpington the initial plan was to issue masks from local halls. On Sunday 25th September, before the Home Office instructions had been received, notices were posted around the borough and anouncements made to church congregations saying that gas masks would be available the next day. The A.R.P. volunteers and Red Cross Society workers found it difficult to cope with the crowds which gathered on the Monday, however. So on Tuesday 27th September more notices were put up, cancelling the plans and stating that, instead, the masks would be delivered direct to people's homes.

On Saturday 24th September - again before the Home Office telegram - people in the cinemas, theatre and clubs of Penge were asked to go next day to be fitted for gas masks. There was such a small response on Sunday morning that the Assistant Town Clerk, L.R.B. Matthews, toured the area in a loud speaker van announcing:

"Attention everybody, please. This is the Penge Air Raid Precautions Service. Have you been fitted with your gas masks yet?

If not, will you please go to the Town Hall, Anerley, Oakfield School or Melvin School. It would help us if all members of a family will go to a fitting station together."

Crowds of people then went to the fitting stations during the afternoon and evening, and during the evenings of the following week, to be measured and registered for their masks.

On Monday 26th and Tuesday 27th September over a hundred volunteers worked at the Town Hall in Anerley to assemble the masks. These volunteers were workers from New Era Laundry, Chambers and Co. (Dyers and Cleaners) and Kelvin House Laundry. They started work at 10.30 p.m. on the Monday and continued, having only short breaks, until 8.40 the following evening assembling 24,300 respirators in 16 working hours. Delivery of the masks to people's houses started at 10.00 a.m. on the Tuesday and was completed by 11.00 p.m. the next day.

While all this was going on trenches were being dug throughout the area , and throughout the country. On Tuesday 27th September 120

Trench digging in Bromley

men - Council workers and people without jobs - started work on a system of trenches at Martin's Hill in Bromley. The trenches were 7 feet deep and 5 feet wide; the sides were boarded and they were covered with corrugated iron with 2 feet of soil on top. They were intended for up to 1,500 people - shoppers or those without shelters of their own.

Other trenches were dug in Church House Gardens (500 people), Tredwell Gardens (1,500) and Burnt Ash Lane (1,500). In the Beckenham area there were trenches in Hospital Meadow (off Village Way), Elmers End and the McAndrew playing fields in West Wickham.

In the meantime the Prime Minister had returned to Germany. At Munich he and M. Daladier met Hitler and the Italian leader, Benito Mussolini. On Friday 30th September they agreed that Germany could occupy the part of Czechoslovakia called Sudetanland, leaving the rest of the country alone. Czechoslovakia, which was eventually taken by Hitler in March 1939, was not even consulted. On Saturday 1st October Chamberlain returned to Britain proclaiming "Peace in our time".
The crisis was over and Sunday 2nd October 1938 was declared *National Thanksgiving Day for Peace*.Churches everywhere were packed to capacity. At Bromley Parish Church the lessons in a special service were read by the Member of Parliament, Sir Edward Campbell, and the Mayor, Councillor W.J. Guthrie. In his address the Vicar, Prependary Relton, spoke about the moral and physical courage of the Prime Minister and thanked God for the people of Czechoslovakia:

"Their sacrifice has been a very great one, and we must thank God that for the sake of peace they did not refuse to make it."

The feeling of relief and optimism was evident everywhere. At Holy Trinity Church, Bromley Common the Rev C.J.S. O'Grady told his congregation:

"Peace has been brought about by the earnest desire of the peoples of Europe for peace and the inspired work of our leaders."
At St John's, Bromley the Rev W.R. Musselwhite described Neville Chamberlain as "a great statesman who has given a lead to the

leaders of the people everywhere", while one of the the few notes of caution was heard at the Central Hall Methodist Mission in London Road. The Rev Noel Hutchcroft, visiting from Birmingham, said that he did not think the Munich Conference provided the final answer to the world's problems. He told the church-goers that it was necessary now to try to get to the root cause of what was wrong in the world and in their own lives, and with God's help to put it right.

The emergency of September 1938 seems to have helped the recruitment of A.R.P. volunteers. Within two weeks the number of air raid wardens in Bromley had risen to 450 , around half the required number. By the end of the year over 600 had been recruited and the total number of volunteers for the various A.R.P. tasks was 1,848, In Orpington there were 628 wardens by March 1939. They had their own social committee with events such as a supper, a weekend in Ostend, and a whist drive. A special meeting was held in the Rex Cinema in Hayes on Sunday 7th May 1939 to celebrate the second anniversary of the Beckenham scheme for recruiting wardens. It included the presentation of a shield to mark the enrolment of Beckenham's one thousandth volunteer.

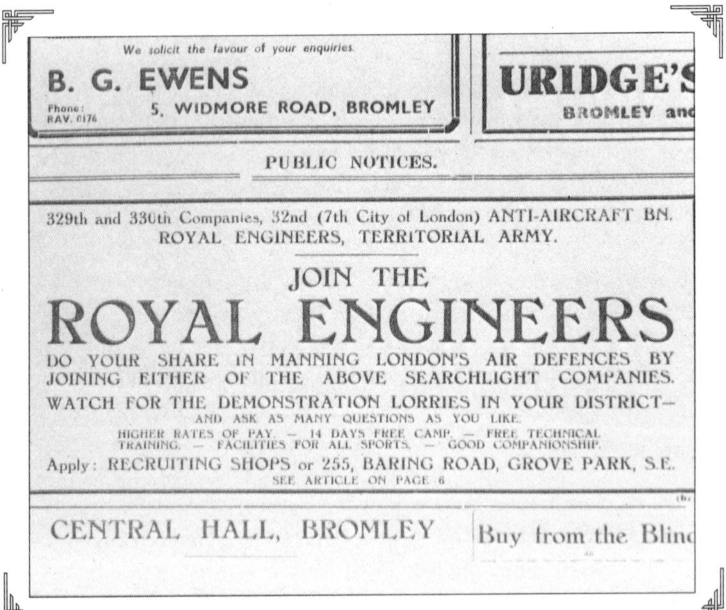

Territorial Army recruitment advertisement

Besides recruitment to the A.R.P. organisation, local people were also encouraged to join the Territorial Army. There were a number of branches of this part-time force based in the area, among them the 329th and 330th Companies of the 32nd (7th City of London) Anti Aircraft Battalion, based in Grove Park. In January 1937 they had just six officers and four men. By March 1938 this had risen to 12 officers and 240 men. They were trained to use searchlights planned as part of London's curtain of light in the event of air raids. In March 1938 they launched a recruitment drive in Bromley with displays in shops, and searchlight lorries touring the district offering "higher rates of pay, 14 days free camp, free technical training, facilities for all sports, good companionship".

In April 1939 the Petts Wood Residents' Association held a meeting at the Daylight Inn. Inside there were displays and stalls organised by the A.R.P. and other voluntary organisations. Outside, in Station Square, the Territorial Army was in great force. B Company 4th Battalion and A Company 5th Battalion of the Royal West Kents were there to demonstrate the use of Bren guns, mortars and other weapons, while 347 Company Royal Engineers displayed searchlights, sound locators and various technical equipment.

The Bromley Detachment of the 5th Battalion The Queens Own Royal West Kent Regiment had 5 officers and 66 other ranks in March 1938. By January 1939 they had a total of 120. In June 1939 they moved their headquarters from Bromley Drill Hall to The Rookery in St Mary Cray. Another Bromley contingent was the 387th (Queen's Own Yeomanry) Field Battery, Royal Artillery, based at Yeomanry House, Bromley Common. In Penge the 208th Battery of the Anti-Aircraft Brigade, Royal Artillery, had 12 officers and over 200 men by July 1939, while the Penge Detachment of the 5th Battalion Queen's Own Royal West Kent Regiment had a complement of 280.

The Territorial Army served as a reserve force to be called into full-time service in the event of war. Despite the recruitment drive, however, there were not enough volunteers; so on 26th April 1939 the Prime Minister announced the introduction of conscription. This meant that all men, aged 20 would have to serve with the Army for a

Territorial Army

period of six months. Anybody who had volunteered for the Territorial Army by midnight of 25th April was not included.

A number of air raid exercises were held during 1939. The biggest was on Thursday 22nd June and involved the whole of Bromley and Beckenham. During the practice imagined bombs (high explosive, gas, and incendiary)were dropped throughout the area, destroying buildings, collapsing air raid shelters and causing many casualties. Thousands of volunteers and other workers took part and crowds of people watched the action, which even included airplanes flying overhead to add to the realism.

During the summer of 1939 events in Europe made war look more and more likely. Having taken Czechoslovakia in March, Germany was now threatening Poland, which Britain had promised to protect.

At the beginning of May the Home Office issued a circular stepping up precautions against air raids. On Tuesday 2nd May 1938 Bromley Council decided that its various committees should:

"...defer for three months activities which were not essential in the light of existing conditions, and to release for Civil Defence preparations the maximum number of officers and servants under the committees' control."

By July 1939 Bromley had received over two thousand volunteers for the various Civil Defence services.

Although preparations and precautions were being given priority, those who were responsible for organising the local A.R.P. were not always happy with the advice and support they received from the government. Alderman Stafford Clark, Chairman of the Bromley A.R.P. Committee, complained to the Council about the "delays and pusillanimity of the Home Office", while Councillor Brown told the Chislehurst and Sidcup Council:

"It's time they got some businessmen at the Home Office and got rid of the dunderheads."

Part of the problem lay in the area's geographical position. Although close to London, it was regarded as part of Kent and therefore not qualifying for the provisions made for London districts. This meant that there were no plans to evacuate children from the area and that the government were not providing as many free air raid shelters as local people thought were needed. In addition to this the local councils were finding it difficult to get satisfactory answers to their requests for approval for such work as making the public trenches more permanent and putting up first aid posts.

By the middle of July 1939 Bromley Council had received over three thousand applications from local people for the government's air raid shelters. Known as *Anderson shelters*, these were made of a shell of corrugated steel six feet high, four and a half feet wide and six and a half feet long. They were buried four feet deep in the ground and 15 inches of soil was heaped over the curved roof. They were free to families with an income of less than £250 a year and cost £7 each to others.

The Council also had plans to strengthen the basement in the Municipal Buildings so that it could provide a safe headquarters for

Advertisement for Shelters

A.R.P. staff. Other basements in the borough had been surveyed and it was hoped to convert many of these into shelters. Fifty two senior air raid wardens were to be equipped with telephones, first aid boxes, stirrup pumps and torches, and it was agreed to press on with plans to make the Martin's Hill, Whitehall and Milk Street trenches permanent.

By August 1939 the international situation was looking very grave indeed. Despite the objections of Britain and France, Germany was preparing to invade Poland; and on Friday 25th August an agreement was reached for Britain to fight to defend Polish independence.
An emergency meeting of Bromley Councillors was held on Monday 28th August, followed two days later by a meeting of the A.R.P. Committee. The plans to make the trenches permanent and for strengthening basements were postponed so that they would be immediately available for use if needed. Three thousand Anderson shelters had been ordered from the government. So far only 300 had arrived and these were being put up in people's gardens. Work on two first aid posts - one in Burnt Ash Lane and the other in the Whitehall Recreation Ground - was speeded up, and all the Borough's first aid teams were provided with special medical pouches. In the country's cities and large towns plans were put into operation to evacuate children to safer areas. Bromley did not qualify for this scheme, but instead it was decided not to reopen schools on Monday 4th September after the summer holiday. They were to stay closed until further notice, but teachers were to report for duty as normal so that they could be used for other tasks.

The full Beckenham Council met on Thursday 31st August. The Mayor, Alderman F. Healy, praised the volunteers who had given up so much time to help. Yet despite their early progress with the recruitment of wardens, they now found they had a need for more volunteers and made an appeal for "level-headed men and women". The Council also wanted to recruit motor cycle riders and boys aged 16 - 18 years to act as messengers. Thousands of Anderson shelters were needed but so far none had been received.

In Coney Hall, where they claimed to have had an A.R.P. Committee even before Beckenham's official organisation, the local Residents'

Association - dissatisfied with the Council's provision - started to dig their own trenches in Birch Tree Avenue. It was only after confrontations with the police, and with workmen sent to fill the trenches in, that they were eventually allowed to continue their work uninterrupted.

By now even outlying villages such as Farnborough and Green Street Green had their own trenches , although the people in these areas seemed less concerned that air raids would affect them.

2

A BEASTLY BUSINESS 1939-40

"War is a beastly business.
Our one aim must be to get it over as quickly as possible. The greater the degree of national unity, the greater the service given by every man and woman to Britain, the sooner the war will come to an end."
Bromley and Kentish Times
29th September 1939

The first weekend of September 1939 was a tense time for everyone. On Friday 1st September Germany invaded Poland despite the protests of Britain and France. People knew that this was the moment that they had been expecting and fearing.

On Sunday 3rd September the streets of Bromley were even quieter than usual. People went to church or for walks, but most stayed at home waiting.

At 11.15 a.m. Prime Minister Neville Chamberlain spoke on the radio from the Cabinet Room at 10 Downing Street:

"This morning the British Ambassador in Berlin handed the German government a final note, stating that unless we heard from them by eleven o'clock that they were prepared at once to withdraw their troops from Poland, a state of war would exist between us. I have to tell you now that no such undertaking has been received, and that consequently this country is at war with Germany."

A few minutes later the first air raid warning sounded. There seems to have been no panic. Some people went to the nearest shelter, others went outside to see what was happening, while others carried on as usual. Some churches abandoned their services, some interrupted them to resume later, while others continued worship.

It was in fact a false alarm, but there would be plenty of real ones in the years to come.

One interesting discovery in the first days of the war was that the Borough's air raid siren, which had been placed on the top of Bromley Police Station during the crisis 12 months earlier, could not in fact be heard over the whole Borough. They had similar problems in Orpington; and a short term solution, before extra permanent alarms could be installed, was that police cars were fitted with sirens and had to drive around to give people adequate warning.

On Monday 4th September life carried on almost as normal. Members of the Territorial Army were now on full-time service and moved into people's homes so that they they could be in easy reach of their headquarters. Otherwise people went to work as usual and the shops opened as usual. Many of them were protected with sandbags or had paper strips stuck to their windows to reduce the danger of shattering glass. After nearly two weeks of war, the *Bromley and Kentish Times* observed:

"Daily the streets have been filled with the usual crowds of busy shoppers, indistinguishable from a peacetime throng save for the tell-tale gas mask boxes hanging from every shoulder. It is only at night that one realises to the full how vastly things have changed. With the coming of dusk the streets empty and a black pall quickly settles over the entire town."

The black-out, which had been tried out as part of an exercise at the beginning of August, came into force on Friday 1st September 1939. During night time everybody had to make sure that no lights could be seen anywhere in case they provided targets for German bombers. All windows and doors had to be made light-proof (extra care had to be taken when opening and closing doors), there were no street lights, and no lights on cars, bikes or other vehicles. Later on the regulations were relaxed slightly; but there is no doubt that the black-out , however necessary , caused enormous problems for everyone.

In the first 10 days of the war there were more road accidents than in the previous 12 months. On the very first day there was a minor accident at the junction of Crown Lane and Bromley Common. Two cars scraped against each other and the drivers and passengers got out to look at the damage. They were joined by a small crowd of people. A lorry driver, unable to see the blockage in the road, then ran into the crowd fatally injuring one man and trapping a young woman. A bystander lit a match to see what was happening. This set light to some spilt petrol and the trapped woman died in the fire.

The black-out regulations were very strictly enforced by the police, the air raid wardens and the courts, the first fines being £5 and £1 respectively for the Secretary and the Steward of Sundridge Park Working Men's Club after an incident on Thursday 7th September.

Because of the black-out and also the dangers of having large numbers of people in one place at the same time, the government banned at the beginning of the war the opening of theatres, cinemas, sports meetings and any large gatherings of people for entertainment. The ban was unpopular, though, and was quickly removed. Local cinemas were able to open until 10.00 p.m. as from Saturday 9th September, although in London they still had to close at 6.00 p.m.

Another restriction was on shop opening times. Before the war shops had always stayed open well into the evenings. Following instructions from the government, Bromley Council ruled that shops would have to close at 6.00 p.m. except for early closing day when, as before - they would close at lunchtime, and one day a week, usually Saturday - when they could stay open until 7.30 p.m. The ruling was unpopular with the traders however and, following objections from the local Chamber of Commerce, the closing times were changed to 7.00 p.m. and 8.00 p.m respectively.

The war also affected what was actually available in the shops and elsewhere. Because of the danger to shipping bringing goods into the country, and because of the disruption to commerce and industry, many things were in short supply.

Petrol rationing started almost immediately, and on Monday 8th January 1940 the first food rationing began. From that date each person was allowed each week 4 ounces of butter, 4 ounces of bacon and 12 ounces of sugar. Buying other foods was still unrestricted. In Bromley 55,000 ration cards were issued. They had been prepared by a party of 130 workers , including 100 teachers who were still not needed in their schools. The next item to be rationed was meat. As from 11th March 1940 each person was allowed 1s 10d worth each week , although for children under the age of six this was reduced to 11d.

The introduction of rationing revealed some interesting figures for Beckenham and Bromley. By 30th November everybody had to be registered so that ration cards and coupons could be allocated; and all traders also had to be registered. By that date the poulation of Beckenham was 66,000. Five hundred people had moved out since the beginning of the war but another 2,500 had moved in, presumably because the area was considered safer than London. Almost two thousand people had left Bromley during the same period but twice that number had moved in making a total population of 58,000 (- 8,000 fewer than Beckenham). Despite its larger population, however, Beckenham had just 526 registered traders compared with Bromley's 624. Sixty nine thousand people were registered to buy sugar in Bromley, 68,000 for butter and 64,000 for bacon and ham.

Because of the shortages people were encouraged to grow their own vegetables, and *Dig for Victory* became one of the most familiar war time slogans. Local councils acquired additional pieces of land to use as allotments. By April 1940 Bromley, for example, had 67 acres of allotments compared with 37 before the war.

One feature of the war was the number of sandbags piled up outside buildings. Knowing that ordinary walls and windows would be unable to withstand the metal splinters and other debris caused by falling bombs, people needed to find other protection. The answer was sacks filled with sand or soil. They were available for sale at 6d each, but many more were made by volunteers. Hundreds were made at Bromley Police Station during the first days of the war, while 8,000 were filled at the Phillips Memorial Hospital and another 5,000 at the Bromley Maternity Hospital.

Most of the work on sandbags at these two hospitals was carried out by local scouts. Over 100 scouts over the age of 14 years had volunteered to work with the A.R.P. They were used as messengers and for general duties, and also helped to staff the A.R.P. posts. Very early on in the war all cubs and scouts were asked to wear their uniforms whenever possible.

In Penge the outbreak of war led to an immediate decision to build air raid shelters in Ledrington Road, Anerley Road, Croydon Road, Franklin Road, High Street and Penge Recreation Ground. This was not regarded as sufficient by the government, however, and the Council had to proceed with plans to build shelters for 2,541 people.

In Bromley they soon reached the target of trenches of 6,000 - 10 per cent of the population - with new work carried out close to shopping areas throughout the borough. In addition there were 40 or more basements designated as public shelters. A purpose-built first aid post was opened in Whitehall Recreation Ground at the end of September 1939 and another one in Milk Street the following month.

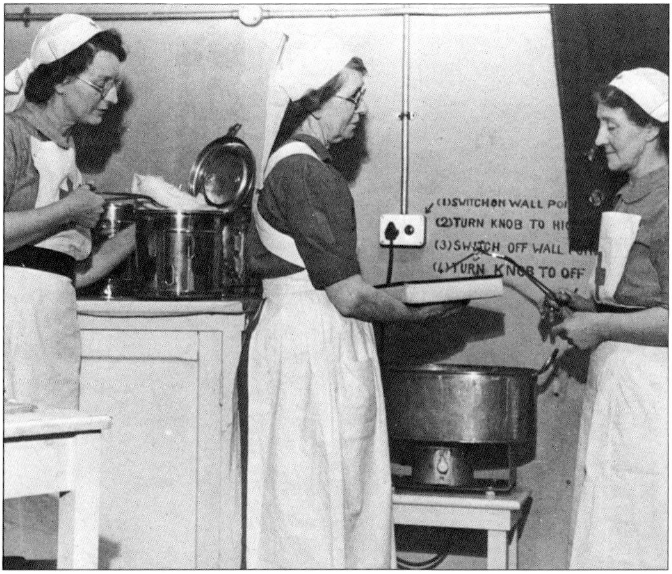

A Bromley First Aid Post

Everywhere there was a shortage of Anderson shelters. In Chislehurst and Sidcup, for instance, 9,377 had been ordered but by January 1940 only 2,350 had been received. In Bromley by the third week of the war the Council had received less than half of the 3,000 ordered. In 1940, when the full number had been delivered and installed, it was found that about 900 became waterlogged in wet weather and had to have concrete linings fitted. In Orpington, although those who were entitled to them free received their shelters, they were responsible for erecting them themselves. One shelter was put up at The Walnuts for people to see, then in March and April 1940 there were public demonstrations at The Walnuts, St Mary Cray, Green Street Green, Leaves Green, Knockholt, Pratts Bottom, Chelsfield and Petts Wood. Eventually 5,800 Anderson shelters were issued in Bromley alone.

Orpington was particularly proud of its Fire Service. In 1934 there had been just two paid officers who were dependent on voluntary help. By the time war started there was a properly trained permanent staff. In addition there were 140 full-time Auxiliary Fire Service workers as well as 70 available in the Reserve Service. Despite this high number they were still seeking a further 200 full-time workers. There were permanent fire stations at Orpington, Biggin Hill and Knockholt as well as auxiliary stations at St Mary Cray, Farnborough, Green Street Green and Dunstonian Garage in Petts Wood. There were also a number of "action stations" with reservoirs, pumps and men at various places around the area.

At the beginning of September 1939 Bromley had over a thousand full-time A.R.P. workers. Each day they worked eight hours on duty, eight hours on call and had eight hours off. The Town Clerk, S. Critchley Auty, made the point:

"We are getting offers now for voluntary assistance, which we are very glad of. But we should have been much happier if they had come earlier so that they could have been trained in advance."

Not all A.R.P. workers were volunteers. For some people it was their source of family income, even though the pay was not very high. In

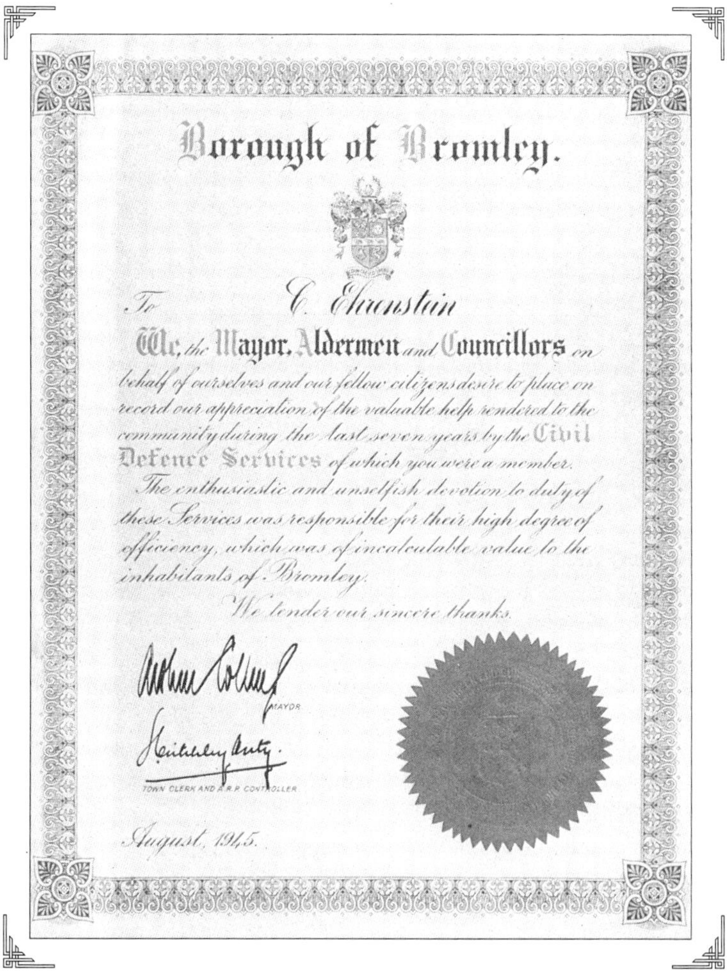

Borough of Bromley.

To C. Ehrenstein

We, the Mayor, Aldermen and Councillors on behalf of ourselves and our fellow citizens desire to place on record our appreciation of the valuable help rendered to the community during the last seven years by the Civil Defence Services of which you were a member.

The enthusiastic and unselfish devotion to duty of these Services was responsible for their high degree of efficiency, which was of incalculable value to the inhabitants of Bromley.

We tender our sincere thanks.

MAYOR

TOWN CLERK AND A.R.P. CONTROLLER

August, 1945.

"Recognition for work for the Civil Defence Forces."

October 1939 there was a total of 1,700 full and part time A.R.P. workers in Bromley. Of these almost 700, including 139 Auxiliary Fire Service Workers were paid. In December it was stated that their wages came to a total of £1,850 a week, while at the beginning of February 1940 it was reported by the Chairman of the Orpington Finance Committee, H.J. Lester, that there the total weekly cost of A.R.P. workers was £2,300.

There was some disagreement about the need to pay this amount of money. As the months went past with no air raids some people started to ask whether all the precautions were really necessary, and others wondered why some workers should be paid for doing the same jobs that others did voluntarily. (They were all doing it for nothing apparently). At the same time instructions were received from the government that money had to be saved.

In February 1940 70 full-time workers were dismissed by Orpington Urban District Council. At the same time Bromley reduced its number of full-time paid wardens to 127. The number of stretcher bearers was reduced from 140 to 90, and rescue workers from 190 to 84.

In Orpington there was another controversy. In November 1939 Colonel Kirkhope left his job as unpaid A.R.P. Officer after a difference of opinion with the Council's Emergency Committee. The arguments went on for months about whether he resigned or was dismissed and even continued after the appointment in January 1940 of his replacement, L.M. Fletcher, on a salary of £400 a year.

The school holidays which should have ended at the beginning of September 1939 were, for many children, extended for a very long time. A ruling came from the Ministry of Education that schools without sufficient shelters could admit only 60 children at a time. Much later this was amended to allow children living within close distance of school to go home during an air raid, and others to go to shelters in neighbouring houses.

Penge schools were quick to reopen for groups of 60 children of junior age. They were admitted, on condition they took their gas masks, as from Monday 25th September 1939. The Chief Education Officer, W.T. Kaile, said:

"It will be understood that what we are proposing is a purely temporary measure. Parents have been canvassed, and any scheme for reopening must necessarily be dependent on the numbers who want to send their children to school under the present conditions."

Children issued with gas masks

In Beckenham the immediate action was to educate children at the homes of parents, and at the beginning of October 1,500 children were being educated in this way. The first Beckenham elementary school to open, for three classes only, was Wickham Common on 17th October 1939. There were trenches in the school grounds which, as Mr Kidwell the Head Teacher observed, had seats at either side with "ample room for work to continue". Balgowan also reopened in October with an "elaborate trench system" in the grounds. Groups of Central School pupils attended in the morning and Juniors in the afternoon. There was still no school for any of the Infants.

Bromley Boys County School reopened in October for the sixth form, with two other forms attending part-time. Because of the size of the trenches no more than 150 out of a total roll of 629 could attend at any one time. The Girls School, however, was able to accommodate 235 out of a roll of 525.

In Orpington there were objections from one of the Councillors in November 1939 that the trenches for Downe School were being built just 50 yards from the public trenches, and that the ones at St Mary Cray Council School were also close to the public trenches. His idea that these schools did not really need their own trenches was overruled.

It was not until the end of November 1939 that work started on trenches at Bromley elementary schools, with Burnt Ash, Raglan Road, Princes Plain, Parish, St Joseph's and Keston being the first in line. It was decided that brick shelters would be built at Hayes and Southborough, and that the trenches at the Central School and Bickley would be dug later.

The local private schools were much quicker to act. A number had their own shelters and reopened during the first weeks days of the war. Quernmore opened on 19th September, Baston on the 20th, The Hive on the 21st, Bickley Hall on the 25th, and Holy Trinity Convent on the 27th. Others moved out of the area for greater safety. St Hugh's moved from Bickley to Malvern Wells and Bassetts from Farnborough. Later they were followed by Baston moving to Devon, Carn Brea to Surrey, and Bickley Park to North Wales.

It was well into 1940 before the Council schools were able to provide full-time education for all children. On February 13th 1940 the Education Officer, Mr Scarr, reported to the Beckenham Education Committee that out of 4,462 pupils 3,073 were attending school for half days, 1,290 were being taught in parents' homes, while 99 were receiving no education at all. Four hundred and forty six had moved out of the area. At that time the schools had shelters available for less than 3,000 pupils.

The same meeting at Beckenham agreed by eight votes to five that women teachers who married during the war, although having to resign from their posts as before, could - on application and at the Committee's discretion - be employed on a temporary contract for the duration of the war.

On Thursday 11th April 1940 Alderman C.A. Elgood, Chairman of the Penge Education Committee, announced:

"At the end of this committee year I am glad to be able to report that every child who is educated, or liable to be educated, by the Penge Education Committee, is now having full-time education either in our own schools or in buildings which have been hired."

By May 1940 Bromley was also able to say that all its schools had reopened. Shelters were available for 80 per cent of the children on roll. Work was still going on at Raglan Road, Burnt Ash and the Central School , but arrangements had been made for the dispersal of the children in the event of an air raid.

Another problem faced the Education Committee in May 1940. Following the German invasion of Belgium and Holland, hundreds of refugees had come into the area. They had first of all been taken to huge marquees in Crystal Palace Park and Hayes, and then they were billeted with local people or moved into empty houses. On 27th May 1940 Alderman Isard, Chairman of Bromley Education Committee, told local Head Teachers:

"No Belgian or Dutch children can be admitted to a school unless there is a shelter provision for these children, and unfortunately from their point of view we have no shelter provision in any of our schools. It was not until August 1940 that this ruling was relaxed.

Although the war had certainly changed people's lives, the early months had not been what had been expected. The black-out, the rationing, the disrupted schooling was all inconvenient; but it was not what had been expected. Apart from a few false alarms and some A.R.P. exercises, the trenches and shelters throughout the area were unused. More and more young men had been called up to join the forces, but the war still seemed to be concentrated on sea battles many miles away and touched the Bromley area only through reports of local men who had become naval heroes or casualties - or both.

During the spring and summer of 1940, however, the news started to grow more ominous. In April Germany invaded Norway. In May came the invasion of Holland and Belgium. This was immediately followed by Neville Chamberlain's resignation and the appointment of Winston Churchill as Prime Minister. Next Germany invaded France, and at the end of May thousands of British troops were evacuated from Dunkirk. In June France surrendered, and Britain was left to face Hitler alone. People had been expecting bombs and were worrying about their close proximity to London. Now they realised that invasion was threatened and that Bromley lay between the coast and the capital.

3

AN A.R.P. POST

This description of an A.R.P. post was written in 1983 by E.J. Pouelsen:

Post 34 in Beckenham was a purpose-built structure of brick with a concrete roof and a blast wall in front of the door. Not all posts were like this. Some were converted cellars, garages or such like.

The interior was about 8 feet x 10 feet and facing the door was a table with the telephone, log-book and record book. There was a clock on the wall behind. On each side wall ran a seat which was convertible into a bunk bed. On a shelf above one of the seats was a kettle and tea making equipment, plus emergency rations. On the opposite wall was a map of the post area, a list of neighbouring posts and their telephone numbers, plus control and other important information. A household register was kept and this listed all necessary information concerning the residents in the area:

Name and address
Number of persons in the house
Shelter arrangements
Next of kin.

On the outside of the post stood a shed in which was kept gas clothing for all the wardens, picks, shovels, rope, signs, oil lamps and debris baskets, etc. Against the opposite outside wall stood a chemical toilet.When householders were away, either permanently or temporarily, their house keys were entrusted to us.
I was a Night Duty Warden. The night personnel consisted of:

A Post Warden in command
Deputy Post Warden
Assistant Post Warden
Eighteen Wardens

The three officers were qualified "Incident" officers, and whoever was on duty took charge of any incident that occurred in the area.

He was in charge of all services sent to the scene.

There were three groups of six wardens and each group was under the command of an officer. Each group was on duty every third night.

The hours of duty were split as follows:

> Warden number 1 reported for duty from 20.00 to 22.00 hours
> Warden number 2 reported for duty from 22.00 to 24.00 hours
> Warden number 3 reported for duty from 24.00 to 06.00 hours
> Warden numbers 4, 5 and 6 were on patrol in the area.

These duties alternated each duty night. The above arrangement was for a quiet night, but if there was a raid the rota worked differently. If the alert was on, then the Incident Officer on duty was at the post

prepared to attend any incident should it occur. Number two group was ready to reinforce those already on duty, and number three

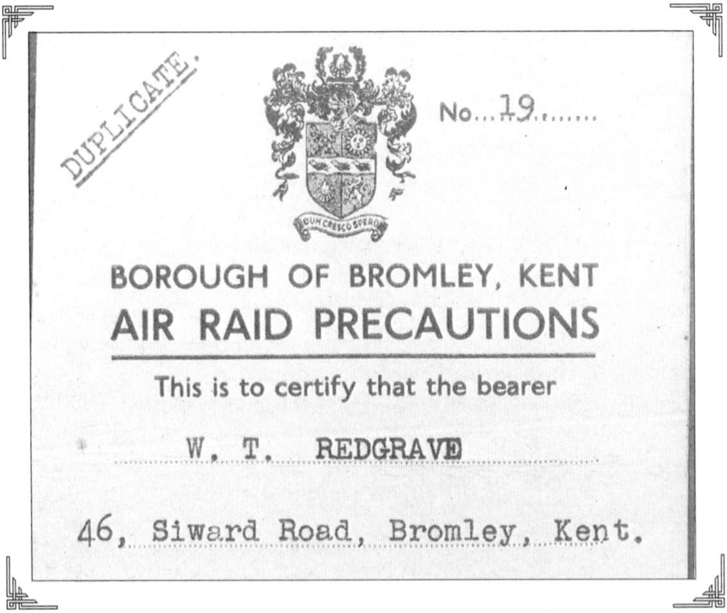
DUPLICATE.

No. 19

DUM CRESCO SPERO

BOROUGH OF BROMLEY, KENT

AIR RAID PRECAUTIONS

This is to certify that the bearer

W. T. REDGRAVE

46, Siward Road, Bromley, Kent.

An A.R.P. warden's ID card

group stood in reserve should further incidents happen.

A warden's duties also included the fitting and testing of gas masks, keeping the household register up to date, checking public shelters, giving advice to residents and investigating any untoward happening during a raid.

In 1939 our uniform consisted of a blue boiler suit, gas mask and steel helmet, plus an A.R.P. armband. This changed later to a navy blue battledress, army boots, helmet and service gas mask.

When a raid was in progress it could be very noisy. Anti- aircraft shells exploding overhead, the whistle of falling shrapnel, exploding bombs, incendiaries, searchlights and flares across the sky as well as the drone of planes. Then there was the glow of distant fires and the sound of fire bells ringing. Much of this was going on while we were ducked behind some sort of cover as we went about the business in hand.

We had our good nights and our bad nights. Some raids only lasted a short time. Others went on all night.

During the 1940-41 blitz I didn't go to bed for ninety consecutive nights. We could only snatch cat naps when the all-clear sounded. It was work during the day and Civil Defence Duty at night. Fortunately we were not in the thick of the blitz - the London wardens and firemen had it much worse - but later we did not escape the bombs, and took our duties very seriously and conscientiously.

4

A STORY

*In 1939 the Bromley Civil Defence services produced a Christmas newsletter with the name **Arpeggio**. It included a story written by Miss R.C. Lamburn who was a trainee in the Communication Service and attached to the No 4 Sub Report Centre. Miss Lamburn is better known as Richmal Crompton and the story was about her most famous character, William.*

*Miss Lamburn was asked to write the story just a few days before **Arpeggio** was typed and stencilled. This is the first time it has appeared since then.*

William's Unlucky Day

by Richmal Crompton

William wandered aimlessly down the road. He had come away to spend Christmas with an aunt in Bromley, but the aunt was an air raid warden with little leisure to spare for him, and he was left largely to his own devices. Time began to hang heavy on his hands....he had done his best to enliven the surroundings in which he found himself. He had trimmed his aunt's tin hat with a length of ribbon and a large feather in order to give her a little surprise, but she had been neither grateful nor surprised. Finding what he took to be a bird table of a drab greenish shade in her garden, and in her garage a tin of red paint, he had painted the "bird table" with a pattern of red spots in order to brighten it up, and had been at first much gratified by the excitement its discovery had caused.

"Well, how was I to know it was a gas thing?" he justified himself, when set upon furiously by the whole wardens' post. "I was only tryin' to make it look a bit more cheerful same as the papers say we ought to keep things cheerful so as to win the war. Well, I think it's a silly colour to have a gas thing, anyway, that ole green colour. I think it looks much nicer red, same as I painted it."

Feeling his popularity at a low ebb, he set off for a walk into the country, meaning to do a little quiet fishing at Keston Ponds. But he found the A.F.S. at Keston Ponds, and the A.F.S. found William. Neither of them knew exactly how he became inextricably entangled in the hose, but he retired after about a quarter of an hour, soaked to the skin, his vocabulary enriched by some of the choicer phrases of invective of the English language. His aunt received him coldly. During his absence she had discovered that his gas mask carrier (in which he had punched holes for humanitarian purposes) contained his collection of snails, that he was using his gas mask as a sponge bag and his sponge bag as a home for his pet frog. She had further discovered that he had adorned her gas mask with an inked moustache and a false beard.

"I only did it to make you laugh," he pleaded pathetically. "I was only tryin' to cheer you up a bit....well, people gen'rally like funny faces with beard an' things at Christmas. I din' know you were diff'rent. I thought it was savin' money same as the gov'nment tells us to makin' one of those gas things into a mask 'stead of wastin' money buyin' one....Well, that frog likes my sponge bag an' I've gotter keep my sponge somewhere. That gas mask seemed a jolly good place to keep my sponge. People are always tellin' me to be tidy an' keep my things in places. An' that box thing's the only place I've got to keep my snails. I can't have 'em loose'cause they get lost an' make shiny marks on things an' then people get mad at me. Seems to me", with increasing pathos, "people get mad at me whatever I do."

Despite his eloquence, however, there was no doubt at all that his popularity was reduced almost to vanishing point; so he changed his wet things and started off for another walk, revolving his grievances, his freckled snub-nosed face set and stern. He'd done all he could to cheer his aunt up and make her Christmas a success and he got no thanks or gratitude. All that trouble he'd taken, painting her bird table (well, how was he to know it wasn't a bird table?) and trimming her tin hat and making her gas mask a little more festive....and all for nothing. She'd even seemed to grudge his beloved snails and frog a good time, wanting to turn them out of their homes. His indignation increased as he thought over his wrongs, and with it a determination to do something glorious and heroic to show his aunt how much she had misjudged him.

He imagined her humbly apologetic. ("Please forgive me, William. I didn't realise what a hero you were"). It wasn't easy to imagine her like that, but he did his best....I only needed now to find some heroic exploit to perform. He looked hopefully up and down the empty road. Nothing at present....no bomb on the point of exploding to fling into the ditch....no runaway horse to stop....no fire to put out....Still he didn't give up hope. William was nothing if not optimistic. Anything might happen at any minute. What happened at that particular minute was that two women appeared at either end of the road. They met, stopped and greeted each other. William approached them out of idle curiosity.

"By the way, what's the code word today?", one was saying.

"Scram", replied the other.

William pricked up his ears. A code word....who but a spy would need a code word? German spies....he had no further doubts on the subject. He would capture them and convince his aunt and the whole world of his heroism. He realised, of course, that he must go very carefully. He hadn't read detective stories and listened to detective plays on the wireless for nothing. He must shadow them and gather proof....it was going to be a dangerous business, but heroes snapped their fingers at danger. William snapped his fingers to show that he was a hero, and the two women turned round startled at the sound. They stared at him, and then separated and went each on her way. For a moment William stood irresolute, wondering which to follow, but already one of them was entering a building which stood a little way back from the road. There, without any doubt, was his quarry. He mustn't do it too obviously, of course. He walked up and down the road, staring at the sky as if absorbed in reverie, till the woman had vanished into a doorway, then very cautiously he entered the gate and began to creep round the building. At one point a screen of sandbags hid what he found to be an open window, concealed from the rest of the room by a tall cupboard. Walking on tiptoe, holding his breath, he crept near and peeped in.

It was a cellar-like room, the low roof supported on wooden pillars, the walls of brick, roughly whitewashed. Several people sat about, and two women were telephoning at a long table. He gasped with amazement as he listened:

"Wrecked aeroplane causing obstruction in High Street.........Several houses in Turpington Lane in danger of collapse.....Fire raging in Hayes Lane......Considerable panic....Crater at junction of Narrow Way and Manor Way....Unexploded bomb in Southlands Road."

His eyes and mouth opened wider and wider. There wasn't a single word of truth in the whole thing. He'd passed Southlands Road and Turpington Lane on his way there. He'd walked along Hayes Lane only a moment ago. There wasn't a bomb or a crater or a fire in any of them. This gang - whatever it was - was deliberately telephoning lies to people. It was plain enough what it was - a nest of German spies trying to break people's morale by spreading lies. Some people were crackers enough to believe anything, and they'd get in a panic and think ole Hitler had won the war, which was just what this gang wanted them to think. It was a jolly cunning idea, of course, meeting in this cellar and telephoning lies to people to scare them. Probably they wouldn't ever have been found if he hadn't happened to hear one of them give the pass word to another on the road. He peeped further into the room. One man seemed to be at the head of it. The women who were telephoning seemed to consult him when they didn't know what to say and passed the papers of lies to him when they'd finished telephoning them. He listened enthralled as the stream poured forth:

"Warden's Post blown up....Warden missing....Feared many casualties.....Several trapped under wreckage....All mains damaged....Fire too severe to approach for further particulars."

Suddenly the door opened and another group of people entered. They seemed to be taking over from the first group. The first group came over to the cupboard by the window, where the coats and hats were kept, and the second group sat down at the telephone tables, obviously preparing to broadcast further lies.

William withdrew cautiously from the window. Gosh, he'd found something out all right. It was a nest of spies all right. The question was what was he going to do about it? He must make up his mind quickly. Already the first group were going out in their hats and coats. He crept round the building and watched them come out of the door. Yes, that was the man who seemed to be the head of them. William made up his mind quickly. He'd follow him and see where he went. Down the road....along another road....and in at a small neat house in a row of other small neat houses. William heaved a sigh of relief. Well he'd run him to earth all right. It didn't matter so much about the others. It was always the head of the gang you had to run to earth. He was probably called X, or 34, or something like that. Looking at the peaceful scene around, William gasped again as he remembered the stories the gang had told of raging fires, blown-up wardens, collapsed houses, wrecked houses and unexploded bombs. And people must be believing them somewhere or they wouldn't keep on telephoning them.

The head man (William preferred to think of him as X) had now vanished into the house, and William realised that he couldn't stand any longer staring at the closed front door. He must decide what to do. His first idea was to go to the police, but he dismissed that almost at once. He'd tried going to the police about things. They either laughed at you or told you to hop it. Besides, even if they took him seriously he had no definite proof of X's guilt. X would probably deny that he had ever broadcast those lies, or that he was one of Hitler's spies, or even that he had ever been into the building at all. And sad experience had taught William that when it was a case of his word against a grown-up's, people always believed the grown-up. No, what he must do was to find definite proof of X's guilt. He must manage somehow to get into the house and discover the letters of instructions from Hitler that must be there. X would probably burn them if he saw the police coming; but if William managed to get into the house and find them without his knowing, he would be able to prove that he was X and - well, no one could say that he wasn't a hero then.

It was going to be jolly dangerous, of course. If old X found him at it he'd stick at nothing. In most of the stories William had read the hero was captured by the villain, but the police arrived in the nick of time to rescue him. He must try to arrange that. Yes, he knew what he'd do. He'd ring up the police, put on his grown-up voice, and tell them to go to the house at a certain time; and by that time he'd have found the letter of instructions from Hitler and he'd just hand X over to the police. Gosh, he'd be a hero all right! He'd wait till black-out time started, then he'd get busy.

Mr Godstone, supervisor of No. 6 Sub Report Centre, was sitting by the fire in his slippers doing his crossword puzzle. He always found the 6-2 shift a little tiring (especially with practice messages) and liked to take it easy when he came home. He groaned inwardly when the front door bell rang, and groaned still more deeply when a policeman entered.

"Sorry to disturb you," said the policeman, "but we've had a message to come round here."

Mr Godstone stared at him in amazement. "I never sent a message," he said

"Well, it was a queer sort of message," said the policeman. "Wouldn't give no name and sounded to me like a disguised voice. Told me to send round here in half an hour's time. Practical joker probably - you'd be surprised the number of them we get - but it was on my beat so I said I'd look in."

Mr Godstone looked mystified and annoyed. He'd just been getting the glimmerings of an idea for 21 Down, and now it had gone.

"It must have been a practical joke," he said shortly. "I certainly never sent for you."

"I expect it is," said the policeman, "but now I'm here I'd better have a look around the house."

"Quite unnecessary," said Mr Godstone, "but just as you like."

So the policeman started his tour of inspection, followed by the reluctant Mr Godstone.

"We've got to keep our eyes open these black-out nights," the policeman was saying. "There's some funny characters about."

He opened the dining room door, and there, kneeling in front of the open sideboard cupboard, surrounded by silver teapot, spoons and entre dishes, was William. He had got in by the dining room window and was making a silent and systematic search of the house, beginning with the dining room itself. He thought that the cupboard would be a fine place to hide the letters, and had taken out all the silver to make sure that nothing was concealed behind it.

"That your boy?" asked the policeman.

"Never seen him before," said the amazed Mr Godstone.

"You've come a bit too soon," said William sternly to the policeman.

"Yes," the policeman agreed dryly, "I can see I have."

"I've not found 'em yet," went on William, "but," pointing to Mr Godstone, "it's him all right. It's X. It's the man what's working for ole Hitler an' telling lies on the telephone about bombs and panics an' fires and things. I hadn't time to tell you about it prop'ly on the telephone, but ...."

"Not quite so fast, young man," interrupted the policeman. "You'd better explain first how you got in here and what you're doing with all that silver."

"Juvenile crime!" said Mr Godstone, shaking his head sadly. "I read that it was on the increase, but I little thought to have it brought home to me like this. Why, he's a mere child."

"Crime!" echoed William indignantly, trying to shake the policeman's hand from his shoulder. It's him what's the crim'nal, not me. It's him you gotter take to prison. It's him what's the spy. I was only lookin' for the letters from ole Hitler what he's got hid somewhere. I ....."

The policeman's grip tightened."You come along with me, young man," he said.

William sat sadly in his bedroom, thinking over the whirlwind events of the last few hours. His aunt had been sent for to the police station, explanations had been given on all sides, and X had got off on what William considered a flimsy and trivial excuse.

"Practice messages!" echoed William indignantly. "Fancy them b'lieving a thing like that. Fancy them lettin' a spy go when I took all that trouble catchin' him for 'em. Losin' the war, that's what they're doin'. Well they can't blame me when they've done it, that's all. I can't do more than catch spies for 'em. If they go an' let 'em go after that - well, they can't blame me."

But William was ever an optimist, and he could not be depressed for long. Probably by now they would have discovered that he was right. Probably they were on their way now to apologise and congratulate him. Probably they would give him some high position in Scotland Yard as a reward. There came a ring at the front door. William went and peeped over the bannisters. Below in the hall was a policeman. It had happened more quickly than he had expected. He'd accept their apologies and whatever reward they offered him. He put on an expression that was meant to express mingled heroism and graciousness, and began to descend the stairs.

But it was William's unlucky day.

The policeman had come to report that a large chink of light showed between William's bedroom curtains.

5

HOLD ON 1940-41

"Our duty is clear: we must hold on!
We must take the impact of the enemy's maximum effort until
our armed forces can relieve us of the strain.".
S Critchley Auty, Town Clerk of Bromley, June 1940

In June 1940, it was becoming clear that the long period of waiting was coming to an end. The raids that had been feared for so long were beginning, and it was clear that they were a preparation for a German invasion. There had been a number of air attacks on coastal areas, particularly in the South East. Then, in the early hours of the morning on Tuesday 25th June, air raid warnings sounded all over the London area and people took cover in the shelters. Bombs were dropped in the Eastern Counties, the Midlands and the West of England and, although London was not raided, it was the sign of things to come.

The first large scale air raid in the London area was, in fact, in Croydon - with the aerodrome as the target. This was during the early evening of Thursday 15th August 1940, and crowds of people in Beckenham, West Wickham and Hayes risked their own safety by watching the battle in the air as British fighters and anti-aircraft guns fought off the German bombers. In Penge a performance of a comedy-thriller *The Creaking Chair* continued almost uninterrupted at the Empire Theatre.

Some time later, on Monday 26th August, the sirens again sounded as an audience of around 500 people at the Empire were watching a performance of *Murder on the Second Floor*. The manager announced from the stage that the warning had been given. He added that people were probably safer in the theatre than on the streets. About a dozen people left but the rest stayed in the theatre and the play continued. The all-clear had still not been sounded by the time the play had ended so there was apparently a "grand party". It started with community singing, then members of the audience stood up to tell funny stories, recite monologues or sing songs. There was dancing in the aisles, and the actors returned to perform a series of sketches on the stage. It was six hours before everybody could go home. A fortnight later the theatre was closed down and did not reopen until July 1941.

The first bomb in the Bromley area appears to have been dropped in Keston on Tuesday 30th July 1940. There followed a series of raids on Biggin Hill, where the R.A.F. fighter base was a target. Forty people were killed there on Friday 30th August and a great deal of damage was done in surrounding areas by bombs and crashed planes - British and German.

What became known as the Battle of Britain had started with attacks on British shipping, moved to attacks on airfields and went on to attacks on towns and cities. It lasted from July until October 1940 and was meant to prepare the way for a full invasion by German troops. Bromley suffered during this long struggle because of the nearness of both Biggin Hill and London.

On Friday 6th September incendiary bombs were dropped on Bromley, causing a large number of fires in the town centre. The next day was the beginning of the blitz on London. It started at about 5.00p.m. in the afternoon and people in Bromley, Beckenham, Penge and Chislehurst watched in horror as hundreds of German planes dropped their bombs on the East End. The bombers returned later in the evening, and by next morning over 400 people had died. Four times that number were seriously injured and tens of thousands were homeless. A number of people died in the Bromley area, including a nurse and three patients at Newlands Park Nursing Home. A few hundred yards away at the Co-operative Hall, Green Lane, the officials of the Penge Co-operative Flower Show continued judging the competitions despite the bombs around them.

The bombing continued over the next few days, and it seemed that nothing could be done to protect the capital. Then on Sunday 15th September 1940 came what is regarded as the turning point in the

Battle of Britain. This time the bombers were met by British fighter planes which drove them back. Much of the battle was fought in the skies above Bromley. Bombs were dropped as the German planes tried to escape. All over the area houses were damaged and people were killed. At least 23 people died in Beckenham and Penge, including several patients of Parkfields Nursing Home in Crystal Palace Park Road. In Oakfield Road one woman , Mrs Dennison,was trapped for 10 hours in the basement of the ruins of a four - storey block of flats. While rescuers tunnelled to reach her she kept singing *There'll Always be an England.* She was saved but died in hospital a week later. Fifty six German planes were destroyed that day and Hitler's plans for invasion were dropped.

The raids on London continued however, usually at night time, and the Bromley area was often affected. Bromley, Beckenham, Penge, Petts Wood, Orpington, Chislehurst, Anerley, Hayes, West Wickham, St Mary Cray and Mottingham were all bombed with enormous damage being caused to homes, shops, churches and every other sort of building. Hundreds of people were killed and many more injured.

On Friday 27th September 10 German planes were brought down over Orpington and Chislehurst and two more in a field near Biggin Hill. On 9th November 1940 another German bomber - a Heinkel III - crashed on to houses in Johnson Road, Bromley, killing one person and trapping two others in the ruins. The pilot and one crew member were also killed. Two more had baled out; one of these hung from a gutter by his parachute and died minutes after being cut down, the other landed two miles away in the grounds of Sundridge Park Hotel where he surrendered. Johnson Road was evacuated because of the danger from 29 unexploded bombs. Three neighbours worked with a stretcher party, a policeman and a doctor to rescue survivors from the houses, having first of all to get past the bombs. The wife of one of the rescuers told a newspaper reporter:

"My husband, myself and our four children were in the living room when we heard the plane swooping, and my husband told us to take cover in the cupboard. Then there was a terrific noise, and a smashing of glass. He told us to keep calm, and then rushed across the road without waiting to put his hat and coat on."

"......There was a terrific noise and a smashing of glass."
26 Johnson Road, Bromley.

More public shelters were built throughout the area and more people had shelters in their own gardens. The school shelters were made available for people to use outside school hours, although not all members of the various education committees thought this was a good idea. The problem of shelters becoming waterlogged continued. About half the Anderson shelters in Beckenham were treated, but this was not always successful. At the beginning of 1941 Bromley Council was told that of the 1,400 Anderson shelters lined with concrete, 500 were still unsatisfactory. Having already spent £3,000 on repairs, the councillors reluctantly agreed to pay £3,500 to have the 500 shelters taken up and re-erected. Many of the larger shelters were also causing problems. The trenches at Princes Plain School had to be specially waterproofed, and Raglan Road School had to be closed on one occasion during November 1940 because the trenches there were flooded.

Because of the night time raids, many people were finding it necessary to sleep in the public shelters. Towards the end of 1940 the government announced a scheme to supply bunks. In the meantime Orpington Urban District Council ordered 250 sets of three-tier bunks to be made from furniture salvaged from demolished homes.

In April 1941 the government introduced a new type of shelter - the Morrison shelter - which was set up indoors and could be used as a table when not needed for protection. They were issued to people through the local councils, although they were always in short supply.

In London the problem of finding shelter was tremendous. The air raids were very heavy and took place every night. There were just not enough safe public shelters for the people who needed them. On top of this there were countless homeless people. Tens of thousands of people started using the tube stations as shelters. Others found the caves at Chislehurst; they broke in, and by the end of September 1940 there were over 8,000 people sheltering there. In October Chislehurst and Sidcup Urban District Council agreed to display notices stating :

"These caves have not been approved by the Council as air raid

shelters and people using them do so entirely at their own risk."

The following month, while making it clear that they still took no responsibility for the cave shelterers, the Council appointed Miss M. Cranfield as matron with responsibility to take precautions against infectious disease.

Later the Council, with government support, worked to bring a sense of organisation to Chislehurst Caves. There were toilets, washrooms, a cinema, a chapel, canteen, a hospital and strict rules about booking sites, noise, behaviour and lights.

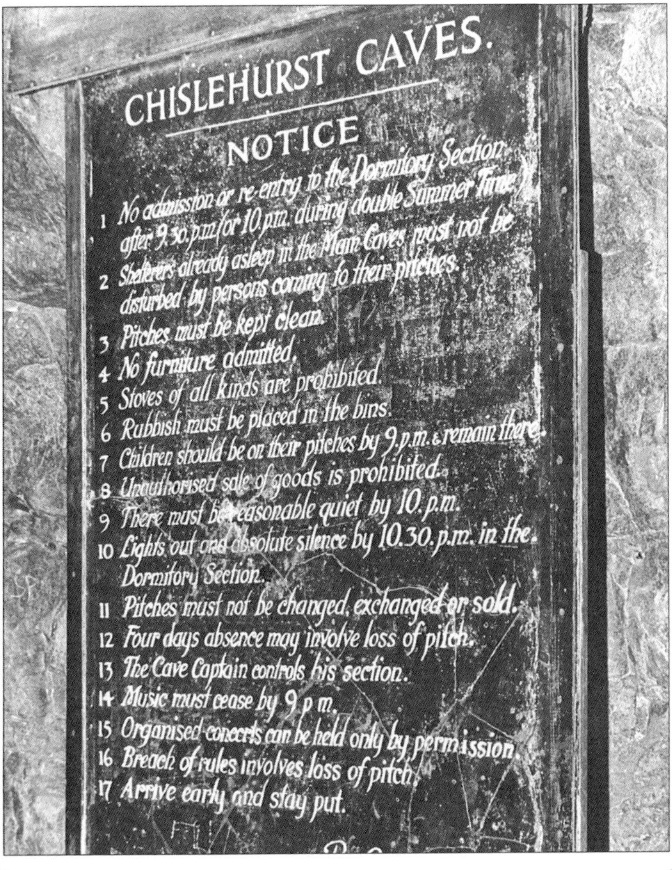

Rules for admission, Chislehurst caves.

The severity of the air raids meant that many local residents left the area during the Autumn of 1940, either because they had been bombed out or because they wanted to avoid danger. There were frequent requests for the government to extend the evacuation regulations to include Beckenham and Penge, but these met with no success until December 1940. On Tuesday 17th December a radio broadcast announced that Penge and part of Beckenham, as far as the Mid-Kent railway line between Lower Sydenham and Elmers End would now be part of the official evacuation area. All children of school age could be evacuated at their parents' request. They would travel in organised parties with their teachers, although some financial support was available if parents wanted to make their own arrangements to move their children to a safe area. Support was also available for expectant mothers.

The first group of Penge children were evacuated on Thursday 2nd January 1941. Six hundred children, a third of the school population, travelled by bus to Waterloo and then by train to Devon. Half of them were taken to Exeter and the other half to Exmouth, where many of them got their first ever sight of the sea. Once there they were taken to their "billets", homes of people who would look after them during their time away from home.

One hundred and ninety five Beckenham children, a fifth of the possible number, went by bus to Paddington and then by train to Neath in Wales. Most of them stayed overnight in a hostel before being taken to their billets in the surrounding villages.

1940 ended with an enormous raid on the City of London on Sunday 29th December. Hundreds of incendiary bombs were dropped, and the areas around Barbican, Moorgate and St Paul's burned for two days. The fires were clearly visible from the Bromley area which escaped almost without damage. One land mine landed in Cator Road, Beckenham. Six houses were destroyed, including St Christpher's Preparatory School on the corner of Lennard Road - and hundreds more damaged. Remarkably only one person was killed, the 11-year old niece of the school's headmistress.

The first three months of 1941 were quieter, with air raids less frequent than before. The bombers still came, however. Bickley and Widmore School was destroyed, as were a dairy and garage in Bromley. Elmers End station was hit. So was a row of shops in Carlton Parade, Orpington and many other buildings in the area.

On Saturday 12th April "Gas Tests" were held in various areas including Bromley, Beckenham, West Wickham, Elmers End, and Penge. Tear gas canisters were let off and the gas warning was given with rattles. Fifty volunteers were taken to Beckenham Road Baths for "decontamination", the record time being 43 seconds. In Beckenham, advance notice had been given, and a number of people turned up just to see what would happen. In all areas there were a lot of people without their masks.

Bromley's biggest air raid of the whole war took place four days later, on the night of Wednesday 16th April 1941. Nearly 700 German bombers flew towards London and many of them seemed to have the Bromley area as their target. The air raid sirens sounded at about 9 o'clock and one of the first buildings to be hit was Bromley

St Peter and St Paul's church, Bromley, the morning after destruction

Parish Church; afterwards only the tower was left standing. There was enormous damage over the whole area, and it was not until 4.30 a.m. on Thursday 17th April that the all-clear was sounded.

On Bromley alone198 bombs were dropped, killing 74 people and injuring 200 others. There were reports of 365 fires, and these were attended by 146 appliances. There were 1,590 people made homeless; of these, 666 were rehoused. Most of the others stayed in rest centres, particularly Stockwell College which had been taken over by the Council, until their own homes were repaired. Thirty four roads were blocked by bomb damage.

The Parish Church, St Mark's, Bromley Congregational Church, the Methodist Central Hall and the Robert Whyte Memorial Hall were all destroyed. So too were Dunn's furniture store in the Market Square, a printing works in Green Lane, Penge, a row of shops in Risdale Road, Penge and a block of flats in Southover on the Downham Estate. The total number of people killed in the district was 144, with over 400 injured.

Dunn's warehouse, Widmore Road, Bromley

Among the dead were Lord Stamp of Shortlands, his wife, his eldest son and three maids. Lord Stamp had been the first mayor of Beckenham and had had a distinguished academic and commercial career. At the time of his death he was Chairman of the London, Midland and Scottish Railway, a Director of the Bank of England, and a member of the Economic Advisory Council.

Three Chislehurst men - Leslie Hammond, Edward Smith and Sidney Windall - were awarded the British Empire Medal for their bravery during the raid. At about midnight Mr Smith and Mr Windall heard an explosion nearby and left their house to see if they could help. They rescued two women and a dog from under the stairs of a house in Cranmore Road. Then further up the road they heard a voice calling for help. Without any tools they helped Mr Hammond, an Air Raid Warden, to dig a trapped man out of a demolished house. Water and gas were escaping and the bombs were still falling. Eventually they were able to rescue another man, and then found a woman who was already dead. At five o'clock in the morning Mr Smith and Mr Windall went home to bed while Mr Hammond continued his duties.

Not all the war deaths of local people occurred in the immediate area. Besides those who died on active service in the armed forces and those who were killed in incidents while away from home, there were those whose civilian war duties had taken them elsewhere. Notable among these were two groups from the Beckenham Auxiliary Fire Service. Five A.F.S. members from the Coney Hall Sub-Station were killed on 13th March 1941 while they were on duty in East London. They were buried in a mass funeral at West Wickham, which was attended by representatives of fire brigades from the whole of Greater London. A month later 21 men from the A.F.S. were killed after they had been called to help the London Fire Brigade. They were standing-by in a school hall waiting for orders when the building received a direct hit. Two of them were buried at West Wickham; the other 19 were buried at Elmers End after a procession from Beckenham Parish Church, where they had lain in state for three days.

On Saturday 10th May 1941 London suffered even worse damage than on any other occasion during the blitz, which had lasted since the previous September. Nearly 1,500 people were killed and enormous damage was done to buildings, including the House of Commons, Westminster Abbey and the Tower of London. More than 50 bombs were dropped in the Bromley area. The railway station at West Wickham was hit and so was the one at Elmers End - for the fifth time! Among the dead were five people in Pickhurst Rise, West Wickham, and six in the Palace Road area of Bromley.

Coney Hall Auxilary Fire Service

6

R.A.F. BIGGIN HILL

The Royal Air Force base at Biggin Hill was opened in January 1917, during the First World War. Its first use was as a centre for testing and developing wireless communications between airplanes and their base. In December it became home to its first fighter planes belonging to what became known as 141 Squadron of the Royal Flying Corps. On Sunday 19th May 1918 Lieutenants Turner and Barwise, flying one of the Squadron's Bristol fighters, shot down a German Gotha bomber during the last air raid on London.

At the beginning of the Second World War there were three squadrons based at Biggin Hill. Two of them - 32 and 79 Squadrons - flew Hurricanes, and the third - 601 Squadron - flew Blenheims. The first Spitfires arrived when 601 Squadron was replaced by 610.

The first enemy plane to be shot down was a Dornier 17, which was hit over the English Channel on 21st November 1939 by Hurricanes from 79 Squadron flown by Flying Officer Jimmy Davies and Flight Sergeant Brown.
There were also soldiers based at Biggin Hill. At first the base was defended by 74 privates from the Queen's Own Royal West Kent Regiment. These were replaced in May 1940 by half a battalion of the Dorset Regiment and a detachment of the 34th Anti-Aircraft Battalion. The Army eventually left in April 1942, being replaced by two squadrons from the newly-formed R.A.F. Regiment.

Among the major operations involving planes from Biggin Hill was the evacuation of over three hundred thousand Allied troops from Dunkirk, France between 27th May and 4th June 1940. While they were being rescued by the Royal Navy and a fleet of small boats sailed by their owners, R.A.F. fighters - including Hurricanes and Spitfires from Biggin Hill - kept German airplanes away in a long series of battles in the air. In nine days, squadrons based at Biggin Hill shot down at least 36 German planes for a loss of 14 of their own.

Wrecked Dornier, Biggin Hill

Soon afterwards King George VI visited the base to present medals. Flight Lieutenant Crossley and Pilot Officers Daw, Grice and Stone all received the D.F.C., and Sergeants Cartwright and Whitby were presented with the D.F.M. Another D.F.C. was intended for Flight Lieutenant Davies, who had died when his Hurricane was shot down that morning.

Biggin Hill's most important and most active part in the war was during the Battle of Britain. After weeks of attacking shipping the Germans set about trying to destroy the Royal Air Force. Starting on Monday 12th August 1940 the base was heavily involved for 10 weeks, suffering dreadful damage, but also being responsible for shooting down more enemy planes than any other R.A.F. station.

On Thursday 15th August 1,800 German aircraft flew to attack British airfields. They were unable to reach Biggin Hill but did attack Croydon aerodrome, where the Biggin Hill planes joined the battle.

On other occasions Biggin Hill was seriously hit. On Sunday 18th August 500 bombs were dropped there. Most of them missed the buildings however, and there were only two people killed and three wounded. The worst damage came in a series of raids starting on Friday 30th August. For a whole week the base was bombed twice a day on most days, destroying or severely damaging every building as well as causing havoc in the surrounding area. More than 50 men and women were buried on Sunday 1st September in a mass funeral, which was itself disrupted by a raid.

On 7th September the German planes started to attack London instead of the airfields. The Hurricanes and Spitfires from Biggin Hill were an important part of the defence, and shot down at least nine of the 56 enemy aircraft which were destroyed on Sunday 15th September - a defeat which made Hitler drop his plan to invade Britain.

On 30th November 1940 Flight Lieutenants Mungo-Park and H.M. Stephen, flying Spitfires over the Kent coast, shot down a German Messerschmitt Me. 109 - making Biggin Hill the first R.A.F. base to claim the destruction of 600 planes. On 15th May 1943 the total passed 1,000 when a Canadian - Squadron Leader Jack Charles, and a Frenchman - Commandant Mouchotte , shot down three Focke-Wulf 190s over the English Channel.

Early the following year the fighter planes stopped flying from Biggin Hill. Although the base had been well positioned both to defend London and to fight battles over the Channel, it was not close enough to the continent to support the D-Day invasion. Instead it became *No 22 Balloon Centre* , part of the long line of defence against the V-1 flying bombs.

There were many visitors to Biggin Hill during the war. Air Chief Marshal Lord Dowding, Commander-in-Chief Fighter Command, was a frequent visitor as was Winston Churchill, the Prime Minister. There were also many newspaper reporters and film directors. Among those who came to perform in entertainments were Laurence Olivier, Vivien Leigh, Jack Warner, Noel Coward, the Gang Show and the Windmill Girls.

By the end of the war 52 squadrons had been based at Biggin Hill. They had been formed from 12 different countries -
including Britain, France, Belgium, Canada, New Zealand and the United States of America. As well as ground - based staff, 453 pilots has been killed.

7

LIVING THROUGH THE BLITZ

This letter was written by Mrs K.E. Izad in 1940 to her daughter in Middlesbrough.

91 Murray Avenue
Bromley, Kent

Sunday Sep. 22

My Dearest Muriel,

Thank you very much for your letter, which took 6 days to come. I am so glad you took the cheque. I went to M & Ss but they have no Liberty Bodices.

You would be surprised to see my dining room & drawing room - beds in both & a bed in the cupboard under the stairs. Bromley has had a bad time the last week & many houses have disappeared & lots of people been killed and injured. A nice little road called Cedar Rd. off Widmore Rd. was fairly demolished by a land mine on Tues. night and again Wed. night. I took a family on Wed: Mr and Mrs & Jill, Loveridge. Fri. night Mrs L. was so ill that I kept her in bed all yesterday & got Dr Coleman. He said it was imperative to get her to a quieter place, so after a lot of 'phoning we arranged for her & Jill (aged 5) to go to relations at Redhill. I had to 'phone 7 garages before I could get a car. So now I still have the husband here & from tonight Audrey Pope, Jeanne's friend, whose people are at Newbury. I have had Mrs Loveridge's parents to tea 3 days as they are in very uncomfortable billets, no meals got for them. Ivy has been away since last Sat. week but came back today all the better for the holiday & some good nights. Her parents & two others were entirely buried by the 1st bomb, but conscious & prayed for help. A second bomb struck the house and lifted the debris off them so that they could stand! They were dug out in little more than an hour. Ivy and her married sister went to Swindon to see them & are much comforted. The parents will stay at Highworth (near Swindon), get a cottage there and start life anew.

We have been very busy at the Clothing Depot, clothing bombed people from all round, in addition to refugees from Gibraltar, Channel Islands etc. - I never get time to mope. I have been going into 87 each night the last fortnight, at 7.30. The sirens go at 8 and all-clear about 5.30 a.m. All that time the barrage has been incessant, and German planes come in relays all night long. Tylney Road got bombed 2 nights in succession, nothing is left - Wanstead Road, Bickley, Chislehurst, Shortlands, Hayes etc. etc. - but Lewisham is too dreadful. Ivy says the 'bus route from Liverpool St. to here is all through demolished buildings. She has also seen Regent St. etc. - John Lewis, Peter Robinson, C & A, Bourne & Hollingsworth, Selfridge all more or less gone - County Hall, Westminster.

I hope you get newspapers and read of the heroism of the bomb demolition squads etc. The New Inn at Hayes is no more. Hayes Station was bombed and new shops there. It is easier to tell you what isn't bombed than what is. We are still miraculously preserved, only our front doors more or less damaged & tiles off roofs etc. - some holes where our own shell noses or shrapnel go through. When I got home from 87 Wed. morning my front door was open, the lock & a piece of the lintel 20 ins. long blown right off. I have mended it beautifully with Woolworth's Certofix & 6 or 7 screws. I've had a quieter night last night - Miss T. and I went down her shelter about 8.30 but it seemed so quiet, we came up about 9.30 & went to bed in our clothes in the drawing room, with eiderdowns over our heads. We slept well, hearing big bursts of gunfire from time to time. The all-clear went at 5. I came in here at 7.30 to get Mr Loveridge's breakfast etc.

Mrs Lavery took her children to Northampton on Thurs. Mrs Brinck still remains. The whole family & Mary sleep in the back sitting room. Aren't things funny? The Gilberts & Jacksons all sleep (Master, Mistress, maid & daughters) in their shelters every night.

Today we have had wonderful quiet, there is supposed to be a raid on now, but I have heard nothing. It has taken people anything up to 4 or 5 hours to get up to town, as all the stations have been bombed in town & some days there have been no trains. Bromley North has been closed for a fortnight. It is all so dreadful, surely God will send us help & deliverance soon. The Aunties seem to get quite a lot of air raids still, but not so bad as it was. I think Hitler has been concentrating on London.

Our baker boy is only 18 but deserves the V.C. He lives at Lewisham & is in the L.D.V.. He has been up every night helping to dig out the dead & injured. They took in 30 homeless at his home, but then that was bombed flat. Now their only home is the cellar. What gruesome work his is, trying to piece bodies together for identification etc.

Lots of the Bromley Shops have no glass now, and they just keep the shutters up always. Who is going to pay for all the damage?

I went to the Police Station to see if Mr Wise was among the dead in Tylney Road, but his name wasn't there, though his house is gone.

The Mayor called one day. I was at the Clothing Dept, Miss Tucker spoke to her. She (the Mayor) said I was to go to them if anything happened to me here - but Hayes has had a bad time.

I hope little Margaret is keeping well. How I long to see you all. Give my love to Andrew when you write and much, much to yourself and M.

Your loving Mother

8

CHISLEHURST CAVES

During the blitz on London there was just not enough shelter to protect people from the bombs, or accommodation for those who had been made homeless. Many people started using cellars or underground stations. Others discovered Chislehurst Caves.

According to stories, the caves were started by Stone Age people about eight thousand years ago. They needed them for shelter and put the flintstone to use as tools and weapons. Over the years the caves were extended by the Druids, the Romans and the Saxons. In the First World War they had been used to store explosives.

By the end of September 1940 there were about eight thousand people living in the caves. By the end of the year the number was closer to fifteen thousand. At first they were there unofficially. Water was available from one tap, there were no toilets, and lighting was provided by the shelterers' own candles. At first the Chislehurst and Sidcup Urban District Council disapproved of the caves being used for shelter but, concerned about health and safety, it became more involved and gradually took over the general organisation. In October 1940 Miss M. Cranfield was appointed Matron. Later Miss Dorothy Smythe was made Shelter Welfare Officer and then in December 1941 Mr Gardiner was appointed Shelter Manager at a salary of £350 a year. At the same time Mr Quarrell and Mr Packman were appointed full time Shelter Wardens. The Council's Caves Committee also elected some of the shelterers as Shelter Marshals whose job was to police the caves.

It cost sixpence a week for a family to stay in the caves. For this they were given a "pitch" , a small area where they could set up bunks. They did not have to stay there every night but would lose it if it was not used for three weeks in a row. Some families would send one person on one night a week to pay the sixpence, stay in the caves and get their card stamped so that their pitch would still be available if it was needed.

The Council arranged for electricity and water to be supplied. The W.V.S. ran canteens and supplied clothing to those who needed it. There was a sweet shop and a tobacco kiosk. There was a cinema and theatre and a church , although the damp conditions soon rotted the prayer books. Other facilities and activities included a National Savings Bank, a barber's shop and hairdresser, dances, talks, evening classes, a brownie pack and a first aid post.

Among the distinguished visitors to the caves were the Dùke of Kent and General Charles de Gaulle, the French leader who lived for a while at 41 Birchwood Road, Petts Wood.

Numbers using the caves varied according to the amount of bombing, but they continued to be occupied right up to the end of the war. Some people stayed only occasionally but many made their home there, travelling to work each day and back again in the evening. Inside they were in a well organised town, safe from the bombs which could not even be heard when falling close by.

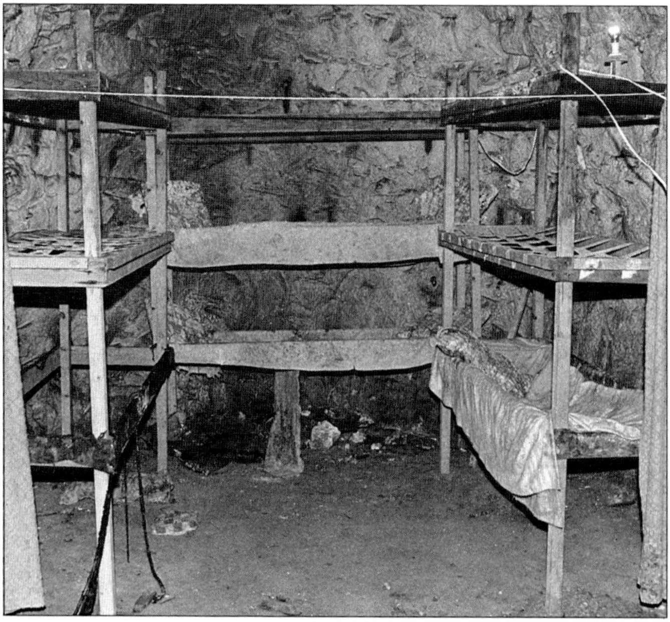

Bunks in the Chislehurst Caves

9

ON OUR TOES
1941 - 44

"So far as Beckenham is concerned we are on our toes and ready to do whatever we may be called upon to do.
Alderman W.J. Sampson, Mayor of Beckenham.
June 1941

After the terrible raid of 11th - 12th May 1941 German bombers stayed away from London. Although nobody could be sure at the time, the blitz was over. In fact the enemy now had another target, as became clear a month later when Germany invaded the Soviet Union. The next two years, when everything was comparatively quiet, provided a breathing space and chance to reorganise and strengthen the country's defences.

The A.R.P. Service developed considerably during the war as more and more duties became necessary and more and more people became involved. Gradually the various groups became known together as *Civil Defence*.

In addition, the L.D.V. - *Local Defence Volunteers* - was an organisation started by Winston Churchill in May 1940 shortly after he was appointed Prime Minister.

It was for men aged between 17 and 65 years, but intended mainly for those who were too young or too old to be called up to the armed forces. They would continue with their ordinary jobs but train and go on duty in their free time.

Their tasks included assisting the police and A.R.P. workers, and

Chislehurst 54th Battalion, Kent Home Guard

being ready to defend the country in the event of invasion.

By July 1940, when the name was changed to the *Home Guard*, there was a nationwide membership of around half a million. On Saturday 10th August 1940 King George VI paid an unannounced visit to the Home Guard on a sports field at West Wickham. He stayed for an hour and a half and saw displays of bomb throwing, gunnery, physical training and guard mounting. He also saw training in dispatch riding and setting up road blocks, then inspected a parade of 4,000 Home Guardsmen from Bromley, Farnborough, Orpington, Beckenham and London.

At first the Home Guard was unskilled, inefficient and poorly organised. As the war progressed, however, it became more and

Tactical exercise, Biggin Hill

more professional in approach and grew into a highly trained army. There were frequent recruiting drives, as numbers dropped when members were called up to full-time service.

The Home Guard spent many weekends involved in large- scale military training exercises. On Saturday 5th and Sunday 6th July 1941, for instance, the Bromley battalion was involved in three mock attacks from another detachment. On 25th and 26th April hundreds of men were involved in an exercise in which a Guards Regiment "invaded" Kent, - with the action spreading to Orpington, Chislehurst, Hayes, Bromley, West Wickham and Beckenham.

With the threat of an invasion still a reality, the role of the Home Guard in these areas was regarded as crucial in the defence of the capital. It was this threat that led, in June 1942, to the appointment of local *Invasion Defence Officers*. In Bromley this job was given - in addition to his other tasks - to the Town Clerk, S. Critchley Auty. His assistant was the Chief A.R.P Warden, R. Proctor, while the District Air Raid Wardens were appointed *District Invasion Defence Officers*. Together they had the responsibility of planning how the area should respond in the event of a German invasion.

In their planning, the Invasion Defence Officers worked closely with the local branch of the Women's Voluntary Service. This organisation was founded by Lady Reading in 1938. The idea was suggested to her by Samuel Hoare, who was Home Secretary at the time; he was aware that most of the A.R.P jobs would go to men and thought that women should also have the opportunity to serve. Lady Reading attended a W.V.S. rally at Kinnaird School, Bromley, on 1st July 1941 when she spoke to members of groups based in Beckenham, Bexley, Bromley, Chislehurst and Sidcup, Crayford, Erith, Orpington and Penge.

In fact the W.V.S. was very active both nationally and locally throughout the war. In particular it was closely involved in the evacuation of children, first aid during air raids, and the salvage of useful materials.

In 1943 the W.V.S. organised a *Domestic Front* exhibition at Bromley Public Library. The numerous stalls included

Salvage collection, Bromley

demonstrations of the use of electricity and gas, one encouraging people to "*Dig for Victory*", another encouraging them to "*Make do and mend*", and one exhibiting toys made from salvaged materials.

The exhibition was opened on 10th August 1943 by the local Member of Parliament, Sir Edward Campbell. Other guests were the famous broadcaster Freddie Grisewood and the Mayor of Bromley, Councillor F.L. Harris , who told the audience:

"If I had been asked what was the outstanding impression on my mind during my mayoralty I should probably reply: 'It is the enormous volume and variety of voluntary work enthusiastically carried out by the people behind the scenes'."

The National Service Act, passed by Parliament in September 1939, made all men between the ages of 18 and 41 eligible for conscription to serve in the armed forces. Different age groups were called up at different times over the following years, gradually moving more and more men away from essential duties.

In September 1941 all men between the ages of 18 and 59 had to register for Civil Defence, but even this did not fill all the gaps, and in December 1941 conscription was introduced for women.
One important Civil Defence duty was fire watching. This was introduced by Herbert Morrison, the Home Secretary, after the raid on the City of London at the end of 1940. The idea was for people to spend time looking out for fires at all factories, shops and public buildings. Although this was introduced as a compulsory activity, there were so many volunteers - over 7,000 in Beckenham, for instance - that at first it was not necessary. After the compulsory registration in September 1941, however, many conscripts were sent to work alongside the volunteers - often many miles from their homes.

As well as their involvement in Civil Defence, large numbers of women were employed full-time doing the jobs - many of them essential for the war effort - which would normally have been done by men. For the first time there were many married women in full-time employment, so there was a need for nurseries to look after young children. The first in the area was in a pre-fabricated building in Elmfield Road, Bromley. It was open from 7.00 a.m. to 7.00 p.m. and, as from Summer 1942, took forty children - aged up to five years - of mothers involved in essential war work. Other nurseries soon opened in Anerley Road, Penge, Springfield Gardens, West Wickham, and Beckenham Road, Bromley's second nursery was in *Draycott*, a large converted house at the junction of Southborough Road and Southborough Lane. It was opened in December 1943 and accommodated sixty children.

Other services which were introduced were *Holidays at Home* and the communal feeding centres.

Holidays at Home started from another government suggestion. The scheme was described by Councillor J.S. Marriott, Chairman of Bromley Council's Entertainments Sub-Committee, April 1943 :

"The main idea is to cover the activities that are enjoyed on holiday, making use as far as possible of the many amenities that are already functioning. By staying at home, people are helping with transport

and also with food distribution; so that we feel some compensation is due, and some effort will be made to provide the type of recreation one indulges in when away in normal times".

In fact Bromley was rather slow to get started. In 1942 the summer entertainments included little more than a series of Sunday band concerts in the grounds of Church House. Beckenham was much more ambitious, spending £1,000 on indoor and outdoor activities during July, August and September. In Penge the attractions - organised by H. Christopher, the local Librarian - included community singing, school sports, open air dancing, band concerts in Betts Park, boxing, tennis, a flower and vegetable show, and a combined display by the Penge branch of the League of Health and Beauty and the Penge Squadron of the Air Training Corps. A special feature was the broadcasting of radio programmes in the parks. In 1943, under Councillor Marriott's leadership, the people of Bromley were much better served. As well as the band performances there were variety shows, a Children's Sports Day at Southborough Primary School, football matches, plays, concerts, a circus and zoo at Queens Mead, a talent contest and fun fairs at Whitehall Recreation Ground, Kings Meadow, Queens Mead and Hayes. Beckenham's second effort was not so successful, though. The *Bromley Times* suggested that this was because:

"Not all of the entertainment provided was up to the high standard that Beckenham is accustomed to and expects."

Another reason was probably because most of the activities were held in one place - the Croydon Road Recreation Ground. The councillors decided that with so many other duties they and the Council officers did not have enough time to organise another scheme for 1944, and just organised a series of open air concerts and entertainments - all at Croydon Road.

The communal feeding centres - or *British Restaurants* - were set up with government money, provided through the Ministry of Food for local councils to provide meals at a reasonable price. With women out at work, everybody working difficult hours, many people homeless or living in bomb-damaged accommodation, and food rationed, the idea was a very popular one.

Bromley's first centre, called a *Civic* instead of *British* Restaurant, opened on 28th April 1941 in St John's Church Hall. For tenpence people could have a self-service meal of soup (1d), meat and two vegetables (6d), pudding (2d) and a cup of tea (1d). In the first week 970 meals were served, and in the second week this figure went up to 1,300. Another Civic Restaurant was opened in Bromley High Street in June 1941, and in 1942 two new ones were opened in Burnt Ash Lane and Southlands Road.

By early 1944, the High Street restaurant was serving between ten and eleven thousand meals per month while the others were serving 13,000 between them.

They were also operating a *cash and carry* service, with people arriving with their own dishes and taking the food somewhere else to eat. This idea - which cost people twopence less for the main course - was so popular that a *cash and carry depot* was opened at 207 Southborough Lane, with the food being brought in from the Southlands Road Restaurant.

Some of Beckenham's British Restaurants were given more attractive names the one at Elmers End was called *The Green* and that at West Wickham was *The Yew Tree*. The Arthur Road Mission Hall Restaurant in Beckenham was not open to customers, but delivered hot meals to factories involved in war work. Penge had a British Restaurant at Melvin Road School, which also operated a cash and carry service, but although the idea was tried in both Chislehurst and Orpington it did not seem to meet with the same success.

Following a series of reports which suggested that many were suffering from being underfed, meals were also made available for school children. In Beckenham, the canteens at Hawes Down and Marian Vian Schools were re-opened at the end of 1941. Others were provided at Alexandra and Balgowan in 1942 and at Bromley Road and Stewart Fleming in 1943. Slow building work delayed the opening of a canteen at Wickham Common School, and children at Churchfields received their food from a British Restaurant. By

December 1943 there was an average of 6,388 meals served each week. This meant that about 31% of school children were eating school meals, still a lot less than the government's aim of between 50% and 75% . Around a hundred free meals were served each week, 45 of them to children at Churchfields. School meals were introduced in Penge schools in April 1942. During the first full month, 8,707 meals were served - over a fifth of which were free.

As well as the recruitment of women to Civil Defence work, there was a drive to involve younger people. Scouts and Guides had been active since the outbreak of war, and during 1941 and 1942 several new youth organisations were founded. Their main aim seems to have been to prepare young people for life in the armed forces when they were old enough to join. Often the recruitment drives and other functions included visits from high-ranking officers. On 9th July 1941, for instance, the West Kent Unit of the Navy League Sea Cadet Corps was visited in London Road, Bromley by Vice Admiral Monroe. Three months later Brigadier -General Lord Croft visited a campaign at Coney Hall during which the Kent Cadet Regiment of the Royal Artillery attracted 100 new members aged 14 to 17 years. Then on 25th October 1942 the new headquarters of the Penge Air Training Corps was opened by Admiral Sir Edward Evans.

By March 1944, 250 Bromley A.T.C. cadets had joined the R.A.F. and Fleet Air Arm. Their basic training in the A.T.C. had been in signals, aircraft recognition, calculation, English, navigation, drill and physical training. The advanced training which followed included the additional subjects of armaments, R.A.F. law and administration, meteorology, hygiene and sanitation, anti-gas, engines and the principles of flight.

Girls were encouraged to join up, as well as boys. The Bromley Unit of the Women's Junior Air Corps, for example, was formed in March 1942 for girls aged 14 to 20 years. Classes were held for two hours each day from Monday to Friday every week with the girls learning first aid, morse code, signalling and shorthand as well as doing physical training. They wore a uniform of grey skirt, blue blouse, black tie, black shoes, grey stockings and grey cap and within two months there were 240 members.

The various Bromley youth organisations met in St John's Church on Sunday 6th December 1942 for a service followed by a march through the town, with the Mayor of Bromley, Councillor F.L. Harris, taking the salute outside the Municipal Buildings. Those taking part were West Kent Sea Cadet Corps, Girls' Naval Training Corps, Bromley Company Cadet Battalion 1st Royal West Kent Regiment, Bromley County School Cadet Corps, No 533 Girls' Training Corps, No 228 Squadron Air Training Corps, No 593 Squadron County School A.T.C. and Nos. 165, 246 and 247 Women's Junior Air Corps. In church they were told by the Vicar, The Reverand A.D. Hodgson:

"I want you to feel as you wear the Navy blue of the Royal Navy, or the khaki of the Army, or the Air Force blue of the R.A.F., that it is a tremendous honour, and to be worthy of it. Think of the courage and devotion of the men who now at this moment are wearing the uniform of the King's Forces at the front, or on the sea or in the air. Devotion to duty is one way in which we may try humbly to be worthy of them."

In all the publicity and propaganda of the war it was always stressed to everybody had their part to play. One way of contributing to the war effort was through fund - raising. Bromley, Beckenham, Orpington, Chislehurst and Sidcup, and Penge each had their own *Fighter Fund*, with special events and fund - raising to collect money to pay for an RAF airplane. Bromley was the first to achieve its target of £5,000. A cheque was sent to the Ministry of Aircraft Production in December 1940 so that a fighter plane could be purchased, to be called *Bromley, Ken*t and to be decorated with the Borough's coat of arms.

Another venture was National Savings. People were encouraged to save their money and invest it in Savings Certificates, Defence Bonds, War Bonds or the Post Office Savings Bank. Special efforts to increase National Savings were made in the War Weapons Weeks held during the spring of 1941. With parades and all sorts of special activities, Bromley raised £450,000 Beckenham £604,000, Orpington £259,000 and Penge £90,000.

A national slogan was *Lend to Defend the right to be free*;, but children from Hawes Down Junior School wrote their own, such as:

"The Allies must win if we're going to be happy,
So buy National Savings and please make it snappy"
(Audrey Matthews)
"Save your pennies for the guns
Instead of buying sweets and buns"
(Dorothy Mortley)

During the early part of 1942 each local area held its own *Warship Week.*

Beckenham raised £600,000 in National Savings and was able to "adopt" the destroyer H.M.S. *Sikh*. Bromley also raised £600,000 to adopt a battleship, H.M.S. *Broke*. Orpington, with £200,000, adopted the corvette H.M.S. *Columbine*, while Penge, with £82,000, adopted another corvette H.M.S. *Parrell.* Both *Sikh* and *Broke* were sunk off the coast of North Africa before the end of 1942, and in July 1943, having raised a further £400,000, Bromley adopted H.M.S. *Zambesi.*

Another National Savings Campaign in 1943 was *Wings for Victory.* Orpington raised £253,000 during its special week, Penge £129,000, and the larger Bromley £470,000 - enough to pay for eight *Lancaster* bombers, 16 *Typhoon* fighters and 14 *Spitfires.* Among Orpington's special events was a baseball exhibition at Goddington Park by American servicemen, stationed in Britain after the U.S.A. had declared war in December 1941.

In 1944 each area held a *Salute the Soldier Week.* Bromley's was held in May and over £680,000 worth of National Savings was collected. Beckenham, which had already raised £2.5 million in previous efforts, held theirs in June and found the enthusiasm increased by news of the *D Day* landings in France.

Other fund-raising campaigns were held. In October 1943, for instance, Bromley's *Aid to China Week* raised £1,366 and in March 1944 a *Russia Week* raised £1,383.9s.6d for the Red Cross *Aid to Russia Fund,* which was organised by Mrs Clementine Churchill "to give practical help to the homeless and suffering people of Russia as

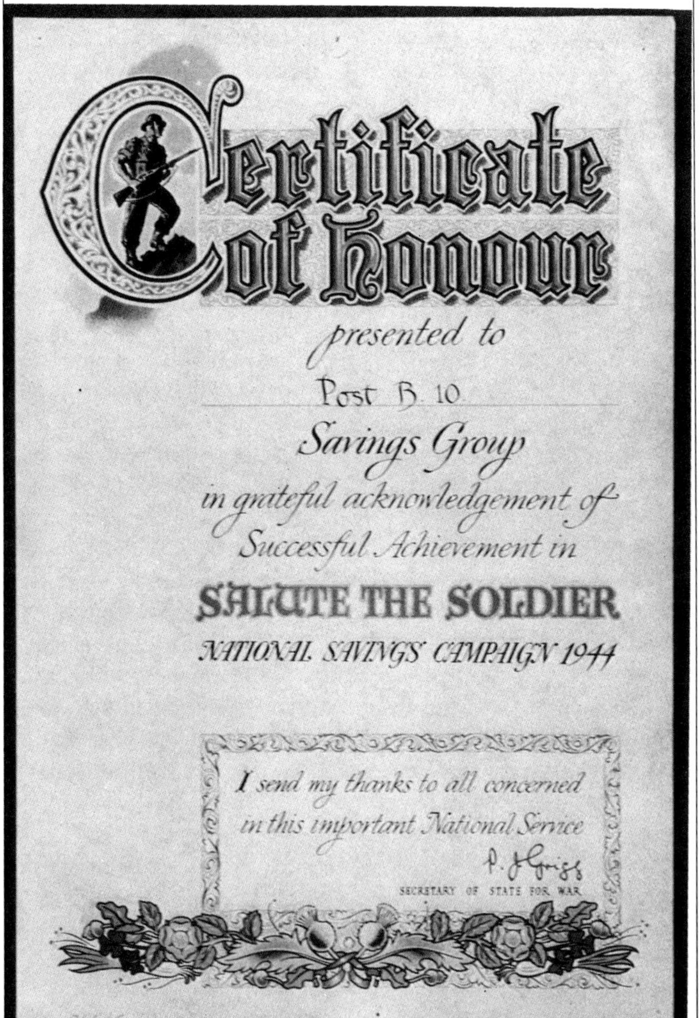

Certificate of Honour

presented to

Post B. 10

Savings Group

in grateful acknowledgement of
Successful Achievement in

SALUTE THE SOLDIER

NATIONAL SAVINGS CAMPAIGN 1944

I send my thanks to all concerned
in this important National Service

P. J. Grigg

SECRETARY OF STATE FOR WAR

266/5

Salute to the Soldier

well as to the armies in the field."

A further way in which people were encouraged to help the war effort was through salvage. They were encouraged to save re - usable rubbish so that it could be recycled. In 1940 Bromley collected 450 tons of waste paper and 410 tons of metal, as well as large quantities of bones, jam jars and tins. In Penge the old tram lines were dug up, and during 1941 and 1942 the Crystal Palace water towers were demolished for an estimated 1,600 tons of scrap metal. During 1942 railings were removed from gardens, parks, schools and other places throughout the area, again to be used as scrap metal.

In September 1941 Bromley took part in the London Region Salvage Drive for Victory. It was launched with a parade through the streets and continued through the week with entertainments, sports, competitions and more parades.

There were salvage depots in every street and special collections of materials were organised by the thousand members of the local W.V.S.. Much of the special entertainment during the week was provided by a group called *TWERPS Varieties*. The group's name was short for *Troops Without Entertainment Require Plenteous Supply*. It had been set up in Bromley at the beginning of the war to provide entertainment for people involved in Civil Defence. By the time it was disbanded in 1946 it had given over 500 performances and raised over £2,000 for charity.

Several salvage campaigns were organised. Bromley's Salvage Fortnight in July1942 commenced with the Mayor, Councillor H. Lynch Watson, starting the *Mile of Books* outside the Municipal Buildings. The first book was *The History of the Great War* and as he put it down on the pavement the Mayor said:

"War is waste, and we are waging war on waste now."

In fact by the end of the day the event, organised by local scouts and guides, had resulted in a trail of books stretching for almost two miles.

The books were all used for recycling paper; although there was some disagreement over whether it would have been better to have sorted them out first, and used some of them in schools or given them to H.M. Forces.

In July 1944 a mile of books was laid out from Langley Park Garage to Shortlands Station, and another around Beckenham County School for Girls. A wall of books was built at the junction of Manor Road, Bromley Road and Wickham Road. This time an effort was made at least to keep any valuable books.

On 16th January 1943 the R.A.F. carried out a particularly heavy raid on Berlin. The following evening the German Luftwaffe raided London. The German planes were met by searchlights, British fighters, and anti-aircraft fire. There was no bomb damage in the Bromley area, but between fifteen and twenty anti- aircraft shells fell to ground damaging property, killing one man and injuring at least one other. On another occasion an anti-aircraft rocket fired from Crystal Palace Park went through the roof of a house at 10 Thicket Road, Penge. It carried on falling, going straight through the grand piano belonging to Mr Hughes, the organist of St John's Church in Norwood. It exploded with a bright orange flash in the ground floor flat of Mrs Arnold, killing her instantly.

Further raids were carried out on 20th January and 3rd March 1943, and on a number of other occasions single planes were spotted. One of these was shot down by an R.A.F. *Mosquito* fighter plane from Hertfordshire. Wreckage landed in theWidmore Road area of Bromley, and the one surviving airman surrendered to a nearby A.R.P post. Other German bombers met with greater success, and during the summer of 1943 damage was caused in St Mary Cray and Beckenham. There were people killed in Cedars Road and Durban Road, Beckenham and a number of others were injured.

During the evening of 7th October 1943, 60 German bombers headed for London. A number of high explosive and incendiary bombs were dropped on Bromley. Thirty shops were damaged, five people killed and several injured. There were several more raids during October. On

the 22nd seven people were killed in Anglesea Road, St Mary Cray, sixteen others were injured and 70 were made homeless.
In the early part of 1944 Germany launched what became known as the *Baby Blitz* on London, although it was nothing like as heavy as the blitz of1940/41. Incendiary bombs were greatly used, however, causing considerable damage. There were outbreaks of fire in Birkbeck Road, Beckenham, Oakdene Road, St Mary Cray, Walden Road Chislehurst, Avondale Road, Bromley, Towncourt Lane, Petts Wood, Camden Golf Club, Chislehurst and Pickhurst Rise, West Wickham. No less than 700 incendiary bombs were dropped on North End Farm in Downe, probably by a plane which had been unable to get through to London.

The *Baby Blitz* continued until April 1944, but the last raid on the Bromley area was on 25th March. There were fires in Hayes in Station Approach, Hayes Gardens, West Common Road, and The Grove. Sixty properties caught fire in Birkbeck Road, Mackenzie Road and Avenue Road, Beckenham. In Penge there were fires in Kenilworth Road, Selby Road and Hawthorne Grove. In Anerley Road the children's nursery was damaged, and Holy Trinity Church was completely destroyed by high explosive bombs. The Vicar, The Reverend Leslie King, said later:

"I would rather a bomb fell on the church than on the smallest home, wreaking death and destruction."

10

TWO SCHOOLS

St John's, Penge

St. John's Junior Mixed and Infants' School in Penge, like other schools in the area, did not reopen after the summer holiday in 1939. When it did open on 25th September, three weeks late, there were restrictions in force. The Headmistress, Miss Elsie O. Catchpoule, recorded in the School Log Book:

"Owing to the absence of air-raid shelters the Government will allow only 60 children to be present in the building at the same time."

The Junior department was therefore arranged into three sections, Section A attending for four two and a half hour sessions per week and Sections B and C for three each. Their time in school was spent doing Arithmetic, English, Physical Training, and Lesson (History, Geography, etc.), with time also set aside for Assembly and Break. There was a different arrangement for the younger children:

"The Infants have been divided into shifts of 10 children and will have lessons in private houses in the district. Each shift will attend once each day and lessons will last from 9 - 10.30, 10.45 - 12.15, 2 - 3.30."

Any teacher from either department not on duty for a morning or afternoon session went instead to the Town Hall "to work on Ration Cards in the Food Control Office".

On 1st March 1940 Miss Catchpoule wrote:

"This is the last day for the Juniors to attend in sections and for the

Infants to attend Home School, as the Air Raid shelters are nearing completion and additional shelter has been provided by the blocking up of the Head Teacher's room and the Staff room."
On 4th March the school reopened "as in pre-war times", with 312 children on roll organised into four junior and three infant classes.

Air-raid practices were held, with the result that the school could be cleared within two minutes of a warning. Those children who lived nearby were sent home, and the others went to their allotted places in the shelters.

By August 1940 the shelters were in regular use:

"At 3.25 p.m. the sirens sounded for an air raid and the children were all quickly settled in the shelters. They sang songs and played games until the all-clear signal was given at 3.55, when the school was dismissed."

During one week at the beginning of September 1940 Miss Catchpoule reported an average of two air-raid warnings a day, and there were, of course, raids almost every night lasting as long as eight hours:

"The weekly attendance was only 50% owing to the number of night raids and the number of houses that have been damaged in Penge."

Later in the year two teachers had to leave their homes because of bombing, and on 28th October 1940 the Head Mistress recorded that a girl of ten had been killed in her home during a raid.

By the end of 1940 detailed plans were being made for the evacuation of children from the area. The school was used after Christmas as a registration centre and then, on 2nd January 1941, the first evacuation took place:

"A party of 48 children assembled at 8.00 a.m. and accompanied by Head Teacher and three assistants were taken by bus to Waterloo Station. There they joined other school parties and left Waterloo on the 10.15 train for Exmouth, S. Devon. Upon arrival at Exmouth

they were all assembled in the Pavilion, and later taken to their billets."

Two teachers - Mr Roberts and Miss King - stayed in Exmouth with the children. Miss Catchpoule, after a week spent "visiting the children in the billets and making arrangements for their schooling", returned to St John's where the 170 remaining pupils had been arranged into four classes.

The Exmouth group was soon joined by another party of 13 children; but in June1941 the return to Penge started, and by January 1942 the number on roll had again risen to over 200.
School dinners were introduced on 20th April 1942:

"A canteen has been started at the school and from today scholars will be able to have a hot dinner each day at a cost of 5d per head."

At that time there were 220 pupils, and during the first week an average of 118 a day stayed at school for dinner.

During 1942 the children collected £7 worth of farthings for the Red Cross Fund and, in June 1943, £87.12s was subscribed for *Wings for Victory* week during which campaign a model aerodrome made by some of the boys was on exhibition in Melvin Hall.

When heavy bombing resumed in 1944 the school was closed down twice as a result of air raids:

"The walls are damaged in places, doors blown off, ceilings down and windows out."

In June the Caretaker's House was bombed and the Caretaker injured. The following month the school was again used as an evacuation registration centre, and parties of children (some with their mothers) were taken to Huddersfield, Leeds and Nottingham. Not all the children went though:

"A small number of children, six today, still attend school but are obliged to spend most of their time in the shelters owing to the frequency of the air raids and the danger of the flying bombs."

The number of children on roll began to rise again after the summer holidays.
On 22nd August 1944 there were only three children at school but by 13th November there were 116, arranged into four classes. By the time war ended in May 1945, the numbers had risen to 205.

Cudham

At the beginning of the war there were over 200 children on the roll of Cudham Church of England Mixed School. Because of the lack of shelters, however, the junior children attended in shifts and the infants were unable to attend at all. The teachers had to take leave during term time so that school could, for the most part, stay open during what would normally be the holidays.

A number of classes were set up away from the school so that more children could be taught. In January 1940 a class was started for those who had a long way to travel. This was held at *Southwold,* the home of Captain McNair Scott in Westerham Hill, which was later used to house a squadron of pilots from Biggin Hill. In February an infant class opened at St Mark's Hall, Biggin Hill for a group of 20 infant children who were able to attend for mornings only and be taught by Miss Billing. In April a second part-time infant class was started, this time in a room behind *The Old Jail* public house. By November 1940 there was a class, taught by Mrs A Smith, in Cudham Hall, a home for the orphaned or homeless daughters of sailors and marines. Looking back, it might seem a strange place for such a home so close to Biggin Hill. Many years later one person who had been a resident there still spoke about the distress felt when air battles overhead led to pieces of airplanes and pieces of bodies falling to ground.

The construction of air-raid shelters was delayed by disagreements about where they should be sited. In November 1940 the Headmaster, R.J. Rogers, wrote to the District Secretary to say that the suggested position was too near other buildings and would destroy part of the School House garden and part of the back playground. There followed a number of letters and meetings involving Mr Rogers, the Vicar, solicitors, architects, school managers and representatives of the Education Committee. Eventually a piece of land adjoining the school was leased from its owner, and work commenced.

On 15th July 1940 Mr Rogers wrote in the school Log Book:

"One shelter finished, so 60 more children arrived at school. Morning school now 9 to 12. 120 allowed on premises at one time. Children who have been working at The Old Jail to come here in afternoon."

This was, in fact, Mr Rogers's last entry in the Log Book. Shortly afterwards he and his wife, who also taught at the school, were killed in an air raid.

Another teacher who died during the war was Lieutenant James Lyddon, killed in action on 25th May 1940 while serving with the Royal Tank Regiment in France. He had been overseas for just two days. In October 1939 he had returned home on leave to be married, had visited the school and had been presented with an occasional table and cushions by the children and staff.

On 30th September 1940 Mr Hickman became temporary Head Teacher. He was actually Head of New Romney C. of E. School which had been evacuated to Haywards Heath. He stayed until the end of November when he was replaced by B.G. Uden.

The school's proximity to the R.A.F. base at Biggin Hill was a great danger. In June 1940 Mr Rogers had reported that:

"People within 1,000 yards (of the base) have been advised to evacuate on account of the danger from bombing. School is 1,150 yards."

During October 1940 attendance at school dropped as low as 16 and those who did attend spent most of their time in shelters; usually because of the frequent air-raid warnings but. on a number of occasions, also because of the sound of gunfire nearby.

Remarkably the school received no direct hit although a number of

bomb craters appeared within a few hundred yards. The vibrations did cause damage, however; the Hall ceiling became quite dangerous and eventually had to be replaced.
More considerable damage was caused in 1944 by the V. 1. bombs On 16th June Mr Uden wrote in the Log Book:

"Owing to initiation of attacks by pilotless aircraft and a night-long alert, attendance was reduced to 23 during the morning, the children arriving at intervals. Dinners were served to the majority of these. In the afternoon the total attendance was 25 and the children were sent home early."

Then the following day:

"In the early hours of today (Saturday) a pilotless aircraft exploded in a field opposite the school, 100 yards away. Severe blast damage was caused to roof, ceilings, walls and windows. The building was worked on throughout the week-end by a local builder with the result that the school was fit for use on Monday with the exception of one room. There are considerable repairs still to be done, but the school is able to function more or less normally."

Another flying bomb landed in the district on the morning of 29th June and, although the school seems not to have been damaged, some of the staff were not so lucky. Among the large number of damaged houses were those of Mrs Lorent (a teacher), Mrs Dewberry (the cook) and Mrs Lambert (her assistant). Mrs Lambert's house was almost completely detroyed. The Head Teacher recorded that:

"Mrs Lorent was released from duty this afternoon in order to clear up damage,and Mrs Dewberry and Mrs Lambert have been given tomorrow off for the same purpose."

Evacuation from the area started in July 1944. By the 19th, seventy children had been evacuated either privately or officially. Groups of children from the school had been taken three days earlier to Penmaenmawr and near Pwllheli in North Wales. Attendance at School dropped to eight but by the first day of Autumn term in September it was up to 49 with numbers continuing to rise as the war approached its end.

11

THE CRYSTAL PALACE

The Crystal Palace had been destroyed by fire in November 1936, so there was no chance of it being used as a Royal Naval training centre as it had been during 1914 - 1918. For the first few months of the war the activities and entertainments in the grounds continued as planned. During the Easter bank holiday weekend in1940, for instance, over 30,000 people visited for a programme of special events. The entertainment planned for Whitsun had to be cancelled, however, when a large part of the grounds were taken over by the government. In May 1940 large numbers of refugees from Belgium and Holland were taken into a quickly organised transit camp, using the existing buildings as well as some specially erected marquees. There were up to 2,000 people present at any one time, waiting until permanent accommodation could be found for them.

Throughout the war there was talk about the possibility of rebuilding the Crystal Palace or replacing it with other buildings to be used for sport and leisure, particularly for young people. Nothing ever came of it, however, until work started on the National Recreation Centre in 1960, and that was very different from the building which had burned down.

The two water towers which had stood at either end of the old palace had survived the fire. They were now considered to be unsafe, and some people thought that they provided a convenient landmark for German bombers. They were demolished in 1941 and 1942. The north tower was dynamited but the south tower, close to houses and shops on Anerley Hill, was taken down bit by bit.

Together they provided 1,600 tons of scrap metal for the war effort salvage drive.

The Crystal Palace terraces were used as a scrapyard for old and wrecked government and Civil Defence vehicles. These were carefully taken apart so that any parts that were still in good condition could be re-used. What was left over was taken away as salvage.

The Crystal Palace grounds were badly damaged by bombs. In January 1941 the Manager, Sir Henry Buckland, told the annual meeting of Trustees that bombs had been dropped there on twenty occasions and that there were no less than 109 craters on the site. Later in the war, four V. 1 flying bombs landed and exploded in the park.

12

THE EVACUEES

Many children were moved out of the area to safer places. These are some accounts of their experiences.

Coming to Exmouth

The morning came when we had to come away from Penge. Penge is on the outskirts of London. We got up at eight o'clock and we got to school at half- past eight. When we got to school we were inspected by our head master, Mr Jenner. All of us went into 4a classroom on the second floor of Oakfield School.

By this time all the buses had come to take us to Waterloo Station. One of the inspectors on the bus told us to go and get on the bus so we walked down and out of the playground in twos and on the bus. My father came on the bus as far as Waterloo Station because he works on the London Transport Board and is an inspector. As we were going we saw houses demolished and half blown down by incendiaries and heavy high explosive bombs. It was an awful sight. Soon we came to the station; we all got off and walked on to the platform and down a flight of stairs into the passageway.

We stopped there for about twenty minutes and then came up. We were soon in the train and we went off. Very soon we were out of town and in the country.

The houses we saw were like dolls' houses and it seemed that human beings could not live there at all. Soon we came to Exmouth. We all got out of the train and outside of the station there was a bus waiting to take us to the Pavilion. When we got there we had tea and soon after we all went to bed. In the morning we had our breakfast and after we were taken to our billets.

Barbara Lambert (Oakfield Junior School, Penge) From the Exmouth Church of England Junior School Magazine, May 1941

Evacuation of children from Marian Vian school, 1944

A Night in an Air-Raid Shelter

I am an evacuee from Penge. Before I was evacuated I used to spend every night in an air-raid shelter. We used to go down to it (every night) at about quarter past six, just waiting to hear the news. We would take books, newspapers or magazines down to read to pass away the time. My father and brother did not read as much as mother and I as they liked to stand at the entrance and act as"spotters". On a bad night it was sometimes difficult to devote full attention to books as we sometimes could not help stopping and listening to the deep boom of faraway guns and the short, sharp crack of nearer ones, and the occasional dull thud of bombs. I used to go to bed at about seven o'clock and lie and listen to these sounds until they lulled me to sleep. Then in the morning we would wake up and ask each other if any bombs had dropped near and what time the all-clear was sounded.

R. Bowen (St John's School, Penge)
From the Exmouth Church of England Junior School Magazine, May1941

Air Raids

It was evening when London had its first blow from the German Air Force. The target was Croydon Airport, and the enemy flew in box formation, strongly escorted by fighters.

British fighters took off from Croydon and Hendon and other places and the Germans soon broke formation. They dived, banked and did everything that an airplane can do to shake off our fighters, but our planes were too fast and had better pilots than they had. Bombs whistled down on the defenceless citizens, and aircraft dived out of the sky with smoke pouring from their engines and tails, apparently shot down. Very soon no aircraft could be seen and then came the sound we all wanted to hear - the all-clear.

Nothing happened next day until the evening. At about7.30 p.m. the sirens wailed again. We ran for shelter to our dug-outs. The anti-aircraft guns started up and the pom-poms got to work. It seemed as if all the guns in the world had come to our district and were firing. Soon bombs were falling all around. Our dug-out was rocking from side to side. We all thought our end had come. In the height of the raid, drills could be heard and the voices of men.

That night came to an end.....gas cut off, electric light cut off, wood, bricks and tiles lying on the ground. But our determination to beat Naziism was stronger than ever.

It all started at about two o'clock in the afternoon. I saw this raid from a hill. I was flying my glider when, in the little town at the foot of the hill, the siren started wailing. Mobile pom-poms came racing up the road behind us to take up their position at the top of the hill. The Germans were flying so high that they were out of the range of the guns.

They flew in, about five hundred in each set. Above were a few fighters and some very low flying aircraft. Our fighters were up, twisting and turning in all directions. One by one they came tearing down. There was a very long lull, but all that time gunfire could be heard in the distance.

One set, another set and another set flew back over. We soon heard the all-clear going and returned to the car and drove off at a good speed. But when we got to the main road we slowed down. Far in front of us, in the direction in which we were going, we could see a massive cloud of smoke and the faint outline of a large red glare.

We drove to the nearest town and found gas mains broken and water mains with flowing, rushing water. Houses were down.
A garage was on fire and blazing like a furnace. We found all our A.F.S. pumps had gone to the dockland area, so we guessed the docks were on fire.

As dusk approached, the faint red glare was so bright that you could see everything. When night did come, the glare was so bright that you could read a newspaper.

At about 8.30 p.m. the sirens started again. Barrage balloons took off from the ground. Instead of one mobile pom-pom up at the top of the road there were four. Over they came, about four at a time. We could hear the whistle of bombs and the distant thud of bombs.

More fires could be seen. One was in our district. As one aircraft came over, the pom-poms gave it a good long burst. The aircraft gave a horrible grinding noise, a noise like a bull charging, and we heard a welcome crash. There appeared a great light which suddenly went out.

At 7.30 a.m. the all-clear blew. We rolled out of our bunks, opened our dug-out door and went out into the good fresh air.

We walked along a drive, turned a corner, opened the gate and walked down our garden.We brushed bits of wood and tiles into a heap and went indoors.

I will now describe a typical day during the trying time we had.

Out of dug-outs at 7 a.m. and then set out for school if the warning is not still on. In school for about half an hour and then the warning blows. We run to the shelters.

We play cards and games or have a puzzle bee. The greatest pleasure of all was to have a play. We had about twelve actors who were called *Shelter Players*. We toured the shelters during a raid and our object was to keep the children's minds off the raid and keep them happy. After we had done our show we handed out biscuits and water.

This is what we did during every raid. We made new plays every week so they did not get tired of us. All this time evacuation plans were being made. After the dockland raid we had a few bad attacks but they were not much to speak of.

Roy Stanley Willcox, age 11 (Penge Central School)
From The South Wales Gazette and Newport News,
24th October 1941

Tribute to Reception Area

We commenced our journey at 10.30 on a Sunday morning. The first part of our journey was by road and when we arrived at the station, members of the light and heavy rescue service, who were awaiting us, did stout work carrying the smaller children and baggage to the train. Travelling with us was a trained nurse to attend to any case of illness which might occur, and a small detachment of the W.V.S. who attended to the wants of the children during their journey and served food and refreshment to all.

On arrival at our destination (until then unknown) at 8 p.m., we found that every possible provision had been made for our comfort. Awaiting us at the station were various officials from the Town Council, the Police, Red Cross and St John Ambulance, W.V.S. and a host of other voluntary workers. Buses and private cars hurried us off to the rest centre, where all were served with a very welcome and excellent meal.

Next on the schedule was an inspection by the Medical Officer, after which the billeting officer got busy and sent us off in small parties in cars, each party being accompanied by one of his many helpers, to

our respective billets. By 11 that night every child had been fed, well cared for, bathed and safely tucked away in bed, and it would be hard to say who showed the greater pleasure: our hosts or the guests.

Arrangements had already been made for the following morning that any who were in need of financial assistance should see the National Service Officer at the Labour Exchange, who would make temporary advances, and for all those who were in need of further clothing to contact the W.V.S. who would do their best to supply their needs.

All you parents who have parted with your little ones for the time being can rest assured that, apart from your own, they could not be in better hands.

Summed up, the organisation was perfect. Penmaenmawr, we salute and thank you. You have done your part. Now it is up to your guests to do theirs.

Mrs Slingsby (W.V.S. - party leader)
From The Bromley and Kentish Times, 4th August 1944

13

THE LAST DESPERATE THROW 1944-45

"During the last few days and nights Southern England has been treated to what the Nazi mentality no doubt fondly imagines is a terror campaign which will end the war, but which, in sober fact, is no more than the gambler's last desperate throw."

Bromley and Kentish Times 23rd June 1944

By June 1944 people were hopeful that the war was coming to an end. The Baby Blitz was over, and after a lot of rumour and delay Allied troops landed in France on 6th June. *D-day* had arrived and now it could be only a matter of time before Germany would be defeated.

Then at twenty five past four in the morning of 13th June 1944 a"pilotless plane" landed in the East End of London, exploding and causing enormous damage in the surrounding area. It was the first of its kind to reach London but over the next eleven weeks there were to be another 2,300. Thirty seven of them fell in Bromley, 71 in Beckenham, 18 in Penge and 63 in Orpington. Something like 1,200 passed low overhead.

These new and frightening weapons were known by a variety of names - fly bombs, robot bombs, pilotless bombing planes, buzz bombs, flying bombs or doodle-bugs. Officially they became known as V. 1s, and in German as *vergeltungswaffe* - vengeance weapon. They were intended to cause great destruction, confusion and demoralisation in answer to, and as revenge for, the massive Allied raids on German cities.

Flying bombs were launched from powerful catapults in northern France. They were aimed entirely at London, and to reach their destination they had to pass over the Bromley area. The British intelligence services managed to feed inaccurate information to the Germans, giving the impression that the bombs were going too far north. Adjustments were made to their range with the result that many fell short of their targets. Central London was therefore spared a little of the devastation, but less densely populated areas like Bromley, Croydon and Lewisham suffered badly.

The bombs were equipped with powerful motors which made them travel at such a speed that it was difficult to spot them on radar, and at first very few of them were stopped. Often they arrived without there being any air raid siren. First, people would hear a low humming noise. This would grow louder and turn into a sort of noisy rattling sound. If the bomb passed overhead the noise would lessen as it went off into the distance. If it didn't, the sound would suddenly stop and there would be twelve seconds of silence as the bomb fell. During those twelve seconds everyone who was not already in a shelter would rush for cover, realising that an enormous explosion was about to follow. Such an explosion could completely demolish several buildings in the immediate area and cause damage to property a quarter of a mile away. Penge was particularly badly hit by flying bombs. In an area of just one square mile 18 exploded more per acre than in any other area. Twelve others exploded outside its boundaries but caused damage inside. Out of a population of less than 28,000 people, 546 were killed or injured. Every home in the area was damaged, and it was estimated at the time that around half were made totally uninhabitable. In September 1944, the *Beckenham and Penge Advertiser* reported that:

"Terrific damage has been done by the flying bombs in this small area; walking through the streets it looks as though a large battle has been fought there. All that remains of many of the houses and buildings is a pile of rubble. Others have their roofs and walls blown away, and even during the blitz no place could have suffered more damage."

The first flying bomb to hit Penge exploded in the High Street during the early hours of 18th June 1944. It destroyed or damaged a number of houses being used as flats. Eleven people were killed and

20 injured. During the afternoon of the same day a second bomb, being chased by *Spitfire*s and shot at by anti-aircraft guns, exploded in Anerley Park.

Three bombs exploded on 29th June, the first setting fire to a warehouse in Cottingham Road, the second demolishing several houses in Laurel Grove, and the third destroying a Home Guard building in Anerley. Twelve people, including several children, were killed in Trenholme Road on 2nd July. Nine died in Palace Square on 10th July, and another nine the following day in Anerley Road.

On 21st July seven more people died in the High Street when a row of shops was destroyed. Other bombs hit Crampton Road, Thesiger Road and Blenheim Road.

The final explosion was on 24th August 1944, when seven members of the Home Guard were killed near Anerley Town Hall.

The worst two incidents in the whole area both occurred in Beckenham. During the evening of 18th July 1944 a flying bomb hit Elmers End bus garage. In the fire that followed there was a series of blasts as the petrol tanks exploded. Seventeen people died and many more were injured. Then at lunchtime on 2nd August there was a direct hit on a restaurant at Clock House. A number of shops were demolished as well as 12 houses. Around 60 other properties were severely affected and many others were slightly damaged. Forty four people died, many of them in the restaurant, and 20 others were badly injured.

There were a number of explosions in the area of the Town Hall with great damage in St George's Road, Albemarle Road and The Drive. St George's Church was badly damaged. St Mary's Church, Shortlands was hit twice and both Elm Road Baptist Church and Beckenham Congregational Church were damaged by blast.

In all, 132 people died in Beckenham during the 11 weeks of V. 1 attacks and 1,085 were injured. One thousand and thirteen houses were destroyed and another16,000 damaged.

Bomb damage, Beckenham, Bromley

In Bromley 22 people were killed. Five hundred and five people were injured, 206 of them seriously. Two hundred and seven properties were demolished by flying bombs, four hundred and sixty four severely damaged, and another 10,328 partially damaged.

The coming of the flying bombs greatly affected the hope for an early end to the war. The air-raid shelters were again in constant use and fear had returned to the people. The *Kentish Times* newspaper pointed out that:

"The flying bomb has come as an unpleasant reminder - if reminder were needed - that Germany will not cease to be dangerous until she is utterly defeated.......Germany's much vaunted secret weapon does not in any way undermine.....grounds for optimism. It can in no way impede the progress of the United Nations toward victory. But it does prove that optimism is justified only if tempered by preparedness."

The Vicar of Bromley tried to improve morale and community spirit by telling people:

"When these creatures come along, not to say 'Will they drop on my home? Shall I be affected? What if I lose anything?' but rather 'How can I go and be with somebody who is far more afraid than I am, someone who perhaps is all by herself and whom I can cheer by my company?'"

New evacuation schemes were introduced by the government at the beginning of July 1944. Most of those who had been evacuated in 1941 had now returned home, but the new plans included a wider area - covering even rural areas such as Chelsfield - and more people.

The entire staff of the Beckenham Education Committee, as well as three teachers from Bromley Road School, worked on the evacuation effort. Children were taken to local schools to be registered. They then received a medical inspection by school doctors and a "kit inspection" by teachers before being taken away. On the first day 386 children were taken to Huddersfield. In the weeks that followed others went to Doncaster, Barnsley, Leeds,

Nottingham, Blackburn, Leicester, Chesterfield and Stoke-on-Trent.

By the time the scheme ended on 9th September 1944, almost 9,000 people had been evacuated from Bromley. The figure for Beckenham was over 11,000. Around1,170 Beckenham children had gone in official parties without their parents.

More than 1,134 mothers and young children had been evacuated as well as more than1,500 homeless adults and children. Another 7,648 people made their own arrangements with official help. The Beckenham Education Committee was still responsible for the education of the children in the evacuation parties, and these were accompanied by a 19 teachers.

Evacuation was not restricted to children and the homeless; arrangements could also be made for the elderly. Councillor Leonard Lyle, Mayor of Bromley, was especially busy in organising accommodation for local people. During August 1944 a party of "fairly active" elderly people in good health was sent to *Hillsborough*, a large house at Westward Ho! Another group - not so active and possibly needing some help and supervision - was taken to Blechton Hall, near Northwich in Cheshire. Another house in Cheshire was used for a group who were all bed-ridden. On 11th August a fourth group, 17 women and nine men, was taken by coach to Waterloo where they were seen off by the Mayor. They travelled in reserved compartments on a train to North Devon where they were met by cars which took them to *The White House* in Bideford.

At the worst point in the flying bomb attack, 100 V. 1s were reaching the London area each day. Gradually however the defences were improved and fewer got through. As well as fighter planes and anti-aircraft guns there were 1,750 barrage balloons along the North Downs, held in place by a mass of heavy metal cables. These cables brought down almost 250 flying bombs, one of them at Chelsfield on 21st July 1944.

As well as the lines of defence, which eventually stopped over half the bombs reaching their target, the onslaught of V 1s was reduced by the advance of the Allied forces through France capturing and destroying the launching bases on their way. By the end of August only four or five flying bombs were getting through. On 7th September 1944 Herbert Morrison, the Home Secretary, announced the end of evacuation; and Duncan Sandys, another government minister, told the press that "except possibly for a few last shots the Battle of London is over".

On the next day, the first V. 2 landed on London.

The V. 2s were rockets fired from Holland. They reached a height of 60 miles and travelled at up to 3,600 miles per hour, taking just four minutes to reach London. The British defences - *Spitfires*, anti-aircraft guns, and barrage balloons - were all completely powerless to stop them; and the fact that they travelled at faster than the speed of sound meant that they could not even be heard coming.

News of the new weapon was kept secret and there were no press reports. On 12th September 1944, Bromley's Chief Warden sent a message to all A.R.P. Posts:

"No official information is available regarding explosions in the neighbourhood in the last two days and it is not therefore possible to give advice to the public. Directly information is available I will let you know."

There were all sorts of rumours about gas mains exploding or sabotage by German spies, but it soon became obvious that it was more than that. Massive explosions wrecked whole rows of houses, creating craters up to 50 feet wide and 10 feet deep. Severe damage was caused over a radius of a quarter of a mile, and the effect was felt over several miles. Yet it was not until 10th November 1944 that the Prime Minister, Winston Churchill, announced that London was being attacked. The following afternoon the A.R.P. Posts in Bromley received another message from the Chief Warden. It explained how the *Long Range Rockets* were to be reported and what action was to be taken in the event of one landing but not exploding. The message ended with the instruction:

"Place of fall is to be regarded as secret outside the services."

By this time, thinking the danger was over, many evacuees had returned.

By the end of October 1944 approximately four V. 2s were exploding each day around London. This time however Bromley was not in the direct line of fire, although the area certainly did not escape unharmed.

The fourth V. 2 to be launched exploded at Crockenhill, just inside what is now the Bromley boundary, on 11th September 1944. Two others fell in country area during September and one during October, and it was not until November that rockets exploded in built-up areas, causing loss of life. By far the most serious incident occurred at 9.15 pm on 19th November. A V. 2 landed in Southborough Lane, Bromley, destroying the *Crooked Bille*t and a row of houses. Twenty one people were killed and almost100 were injured. *The Crooked Billet* was regularly used on Saturday nights by the R.A.F. from Biggin Hill, who often worried local residents by leaving their car lights on in the car park. The V. 2 struck on a Sunday, convincing people that information had been supplied by a German spy who got the wrong day.

In December 1944 six people died in Jevington Way, Mottingham, and on 14th January 1945 seven people died in an explosion which demolished six houses in Court Road, Orpington. On 9th February, four people died in West Common Road, Hayes. The explosion destroyed two shops, five houses and a nursery garden. It also damaged the Parish Church, the Village Hall, a public house, a garage, a school, 13 shops and nearly 300 houses. On the same day a V. 2 rocket hit Walden Avenue in Chislehurst, killing two people and injuring 50. Eight houses were destroyed and 350 were damaged, as were six shops, a public house and a church. In the very early hours of 15th March 1945, two large houses were hit in Crystal Palace Park Road. Eight people were killed, although it was not until two days later that the last body was recovered.

Altogether approximately thirty V. 2s exploded in the Bromley area. These included the last one of the war which landed in Court Road, Orpington at around 5.00 p.m. on 27th March 1945. Fourteen homes were destroyed, one person was killed and seventy were injured. The next day a V. 1 flying bomb exploded in Scadbury Park, Chislehurst, causing the last air raid casualties of the war.

The National Savings fund- raising efforts continued despite the raids. *A Salute the Soldier Week* raised £120,000 in Penge and Anerley at the beginning of July1944, even though the V. 1s prevented the organisation of many functions. The fact that the week happened at all was quite remarkable, and won a great deal of praise for the organising committee. Lord Kindersley, President of the National Savings Movement, wrote:

"I feel certain that your residents will sieze the opportunity offered by Salute the Soldier Week not only to prove to Germany that this blind barbarity enormously intensifies our will to win, but to make clear to our soldiers that nothing can shake our determination to show our gratitude and admiration of their undaunted courage and sacrifices."

A similar week in Orpington at about the same time raised just over £250,000 in National Savings, reckoned to be enough to meet the cost of maintaining an army base hospital for a year. Over £4,000 was raised in Bromley's *Naval Week* at the end of October 1944, when the attraction included a "doodle-bug exhibition" in a High Street shop.

Although the V. 1s and V. 2s were a terrible and horrifying setback people realised, or at least hoped, that the raids were a desperate attempt by the German Command to delay the end of the war and to extend the suffering. The war was going on for longer than they had expected, but they knew that the end was in sight. Conversation and official debate was about what life would be like after the war.

Certainly one of the biggest problems would be housing. In November 1944 a report to Penge Urban District Council revealed that 104 houses had already been demolished and another 369 were due to follow. There were 867 houses which were seriously damaged and uninhabitable. People were still living in 2,566 houses which were regarded as seriously damaged, while almost another 2,000 were still slightly damaged. There were over 1,000 men from different parts of the country working on the repairs.

The short-term answer to the housing crisis was regarded as being prefabricated dwellings. In February 1945 Bromley Council ordered a large number of *Portal* homes from the government. These were to be supplied by the Ministry of Works complete with cookers, washing boilers and refrigerators. The planned sites were Crown Lane, Magpie Hall Lane, Turpington Lane, Link Way, Homemead Road, Mead Way and Bourne Vale.

A sign that the war was nearly over came with the order in November 1944 for the Home Guard battalions to "stand down". Two months earlier the 51st Kent Battalion had been inspected at Queens Mead by Field Marshal The Viscount Gort, V.C., G.C.B., C.B.E., D.S.O., M.V.O., M.C., A.D.C., who had spoken about:

"....the great reputation this Battalion holds for extending the helping hand not only to the Civil Defence, but also to the general public in an area which has suffered sad and serious devastation."

On the announcement of the stand-down the 51st Battalion immediately established a *Home Guard Association* to keep the contacts that had been made during the war. Among the other local Home Guards to take part in stand-down parades on the morning of Sunday 3rd December 1944 were the 52nd Kent Battalion at Farnborough, the 55th Kent Battalion at West Wickham, the 19th County of London (South Suburban Gas Company) Battalion at St Mary Cray, the101st Home Guard Rocket A.A. Battery, and the D (Penge) Company of the 57th County of London Battalion. During the afternoon of the same day, local representatives were among the 7,000 parading past H.M. King George VI in Hyde Park. With the King and Queen was the Lord Mayor of London, Sir Frank Alexander, himself a private in the Bromley Home Guard. In March 1945 the part-time firemen stood down from the National Fire Service.

A dinner was held at *The White Hart* on Friday 16th March, and the *Bromley PTF Association* was formed. Two days later over 50 from Bromley and District joined others in a parade in Hyde Park inspected by the Home Secretary, Herbert Morrison.

The Civil Defence Services had been drastically cut back at the end of 1944. In Bromley the Town Clerk, S. Critchley Auty, wrote to all workers who:

"..... night after night and day after day throughout these five long years have manned the Depots, Posts, Centres and Communications; watched for the falling bombs; reported casualties, fire and damage; sought for the trapped; rescued the buried; rendered first aid; conveyed the casualties to Posts and Hospitals; dressed the wounds; extinguished incipient fires; warned the Public Service Companies - Gas, Electricity, Water, Telephones and Railways; recovered and cared for the dead; identified the casualties; operated the Rest and Medical Rest Centres, the Information Bureaux, the Emergency Feeding Centres and Canteens; transported the old and the infirm; prepared against gas; cleared and restored the roads and lighted obstacles; effected repairs to houses; removed and stored furniture; recovered and safeguarded valuables; rehoused and billeted the homeless; provided and maintained the shelters and promoted the welfare of those using them - in fact to every member of the Civil Defence Services of Bromley I send a heartfelt "WELL DONE". You have been weary at times but you have not faltered; you may have been afraid but you have not flinched."

Now it really was just a matter of waiting for the end as the Allied troops came closer to victory in Europe.

14

FLYING BOMB ON BECKENHAM

This flying bomb incident was recalled by E.J. Pouelsen in 1980

On Friday 4th August 1944 I was at work in Croydon. The doodle-bugs had been coming over at intervals, and shortly after one explosion in the late afternoon I had a phone call to go home to Cherry Tree Walk in Beckenham as my house had been damaged.

All the way home I was full of apprehension as to what I would find. Coming to the corner of my road, at first glance it didn't seem to be too bad. But it was a different story when I went inside.

Windows empty, curtains tattered and torn, and the hall and stairs covered with plaster. Glass, torn wallpaper, everything crunching underfoot. From here into the lounge not too bad. Some plaster down plus dust and dirt. Into the dining room. No ceiling. Patches of bare brick. Lamp bowl hanging from one chain - unbroken. Drawers pulled out by the blast. Doors swinging open and the French windows flat on the lawn. Everything covered with soot, dirt and plaster. A pile of roof tiles outside. A pair of slacks hanging on a line just outside vanished, never to be seen again.

Couldn't get into the kitchen as the door was jammed. Out into the garden. The shed gone and the garage just a heap of timber and asbestos. Fences flat and broken, and glass and tiles everywhere. Looking up, the back half of the roof was missing and tattered curtains were hanging from empty windows.

The back door had been thrown up against the kitchen door which was why it was jammed. The gas, water and electricity were still O.K. but again the old story of dirt, dust and plaster.

Upstairs to the bathroom to find the bath, handbasin and lavatory full of plaster, tiles and broken wood from the roof - but only two or three wall tiles out.

The back bedroom was the same story but the front bedroom was really laughable. The ceiling had come down in one complete piece, and where it had hit the furniture it had split and hung down over the sides and top, just like dust sheets - dirty and grey.

The scene all around was the same, but nearer the crater the greater the damage. Our house was approximately fifty yards away.

The Civil Defence were busy and so were the Local Authority officers, taking particulars and giving help.

Now we had to get busy and clear a space in the lounge to eat and sleep, ready for the clean-up in the morning. All that night loose bits of plaster would plonk on the stairs and floors.

The next morning lorries turned up with tiles, glass and timber, and working parties from the Forces. All around the sounds of shovels, brooms, getting things shipshape. Outside the houses the piles of rubbish got bigger and bigger, and at the finish the pile was topped with a broken lavatory pan.

On the Monday morning, while the working parties were repairing the roofs, the warning went again and all of a sudden they all disappeared like rabbits down a hole - with a head showing out of a shelter. Looking up I saw a doodle-bug buzzing across the sky, flat out and going for miles. On questioning them they said it was their first experience of a doodle-bug and they didn't know what to expect.

In my own home I had fixed the ceiling walls etc. with *Sisalcraft* and laths, and we lived like this until 1946 when it was possible to have the job done properly.

E.J. Pouelsen 1980

15

THE PERIL HAS PASSED
1945 - 46

"We have looked into the eyes of danger and death; but the peril has passed, and we may be proud to have held the fortress of Britain in the noblest hour of her history."
Beckenham and Penge Advertiser, May 10th 1945

The wait for the end of the war seemed to go on for ever. Then by the beginning of May 1945 an announcement was expected any day. In Bromley the Council had already prepared a programme of special events, and copies of a souvenir brochure were delivered by the Women's Voluntary Service to every house in the Borough. In Beckenham all the flagpoles were repaired and new ones were put up.

On Saturday 5th May everybody was sure that the news would be released, but nothing happened. Again on the Sunday everything was quiet. Then at seven o'clock in the evening of Monday 7th May came the report that Germany had agreed to an unconditional surrender. The next day was to be *Victory in Europe (VE) Day*. The Prime Minister would speak on the radio at three o' clock in the afternoon and the King would broadcast at nine o' clock in the evening.

Immediately, the flags started to appear. In Beckenham, the Town Hall and St George's Church were both floodlit. The biggest celebrations were in Penge. Bonfires were lit on many of the bombsites, where people sang and danced well into the night. Others danced through the High Street, and it was only a thunderstorm around midnight which brought the parties to an end.

Except for one short shower VE Day, Tuesday 10th May, was sunny and hot. Everything stayed closed except for food shops which opened briefly during the morning. Shops, offices and houses throughout the area were decorated with flags and streamers, and loudspeakers in the streets played music and recordings of church bells. Crowds gathered in the streets and the parks, many of the people carrying flags and some of them dressed in red, white and blue.

Perhaps the biggest crowd was in Bromley Market Square where hundreds of people heard the Prime Minister's radio speech over the loudspeakers.

Churches everywhere held special services during the evening, and at some of them the congregations stayed behind to listen to the King's broadcast. The festivities carried on with music and dancing in the parks. In Queen's Mead there was community singing led by T. Ratcliff, who was famous for leading the singing before the F.A. Cup Finals at Wembley.

After dark there were more bonfires. In Penge there were even more than the night before. According to the *Beckenham and Penge Advertiser:*

"Tuesday, in very truth, provided a night of nights, with people disporting themselves everywhere in gay abandon. Dancing, singing and revelry in the streets went on half-way through the night, many not returning to their homes till 2 a.m. and even later. "

One of the biggest bonfires was at the Bromley Fire Brigade headquarters at Quernmore. Fire officers in Beckenham also had their own bonfire but had to leave it to attend a call in Mackenzie Road. Fireworks were let off in various places and many buildings - such as the Municipal Buildings, the Parish Church tower and Medhurst's store - in Bromley were floodlit.

A bonfire in Palace View, Bromley attracted a crowd of two hundred. A life- size model of Adolf Hitler was hanged and then thrown onto the fire in the middle of the road. There was dancing in the street and then an open-air film show.

Earlier in the day, one of the first children's street parties was held in Chatsworth Avenue. Tables were set up in the street and thirty five children from Chatsworth Avenue and Burnt Ash Lane sat down to a tea of sandwiches, cakes, jellies and lemonade. Afterwards there were games followed by yet another bonfire.

Wednesday 9th May was known as *VE plus 1*. Thousands of people went to Queens Mead for an open-air service. At 10.30 a.m. a procession left the Municipal Buildings in Widmore Road .Led by the Salvation Army band and consisting of the Mayor, Councillors, Justices of the Peace, and Ministers of the various churches. They arrived at Queens Mead for the service at 11 o'clock. The singing was accompanied by both the Salvation Army band and the Home Guard band, and was led by Bromley Male Voice Choir. The service was conducted by the Vicar of Bromley, the Reverand Murray Walton, and The Reverend O. G. Whitfield, Minister of Bromley Congregational Church. The lessons were read by the Mayor of Bromley, Councillor Arthur Collins, and Sir Edward Campbell M.P.

On the same day, local children were invited to free entertainments at the *Gaumont* and *Odeon* cinemas in Bromley and the *Rex* in Hayes.

Thursday 10th May - *VE plus 2* - was "children's day". The schools reopened with a short service, and there were sports and games through the rest of the day.

The festivities continued for quite some time. Children's street parties were held in many areas, especially on Saturday 12th May. As well as the food there were usually games, entertainments and competitions. In Borkwood Way, Farnborough the prizes were presented by Ronnie Mitchell, a sailor who had arrived home that day after three and a half years in German prisoner of war camps.

One of the biggest street parties was in Shortlands where 150 children, from the area around Meadow Road, Martins Road, Beckenham Lane and Shortlands Gardens, joined in the fun. After tea they were entertained by a ventriloquist and then took part in races. Later there was a dance and a bonfire for the adults. There was also a dance in Addison Road, Bromley. It followed the children's party on Friday afternoon and went on well into the early hours of Saturday.

Children's street party, Beckenham

Some of the parties were affected by showers. In Penge the children of Clarina Road, Evelina Road and Croydon Road had their party under the canopy of the *Penge Empire* theatre, while the hundred children at the Phoenix Road street party had to move into the mission hall in Mosslea Road.

More services were held on Sunday 13th May, *Victory Thanksgiving Day*. In Bromley the Mayor stood on the steps of the Municipal Buildings to take the salute of an enormous parade on its way to a special service at the *Gaumont* cinema. In the parade were representatives of Police, Royal Artillery, Royal Air Force, Home Guard, Cadet forces, British Legion, Red Cross, scouts, guides, Civil Defence Workers, Women's Voluntary Service and others. The parade was so long that as the front was arriving at the cinema, the other end was only just starting off from Palace Grove. Two thousand people were at the service which was conducted by The Reverend Captain G. R. New.

Throughout all the celebrations there was still time for sadness, as people remembered not only what they had suffered but also all those who had been injured or killed in five and a half years of war. There was also the realisation that although Germany had surrendered, Britain was still at war with Japan. In his VE Day message the Mayor of Bromley, Councillor Arthur Collins, had said:

"This is no time for jubilation, though we may relax for a day. The war is not yet over. One contest has been won, and at a great price. The last stage, out in the far Pacific Ocean, is now entered, calling us all to further sacrifice and service, and this call will surely keep us steady, thoughtful and subdued, as we enjoy our brief respite from work this memorable day."

When Japan finally surrendered at midnight on Tuesday 14th August 1945 the Bromley area, like many others throughout the country, was unprepared. No plans had been made to celebrate *VJ Day,* and although the shops closed and some flags appeared things were very quiet compared with what had happened in May.

The official festivities were saved for June 1946. Whitsun weekend 8th-10th June was a time of national "Peace Celebrations". On the

Saturday afternoon thousands of children and their parents went to a free funfair and tea party at Queen's Mead in Bromley despite the heavy rain. The weather meant that the Sunday service planned for the Church House grounds was held inside the temporary Parish Church. By Monday evening it had cleared up ready for a spectacular firework display on Martins Hill.

There were also fireworks at Orpington Sports Club in Goddington Lane, but most of Orpington's street parties had to be cancelled. In Chislehurst and Mottingham all the available halls were used to serve teas to 1,500 children who had been expecting an enormous picnic. In Coney Hall the children were treated to an afternoon of watching television. Victory Queens were crowned in Locksbottom and Cudham, and elsewhere there were band concerts, sports days, baby shows, competitions and dances.

Most of the activities were for children. Many of the adults were not so keen to celebrate. The usual processions were missing and there were not many street decorations. The war was over, but there was still a great deal for people to worry about. In 1945 Councillor Collins had written:

"Let us then consider now how best we may serve our nation and our local community, not just ourselves. So as our men come home we may help them to build a kingdom worthy of them, the living, and of their comrades who will never return."

Now shortages of food, fuel and all sorts of other goods still made rationing and long queues a part of normal everyday life; and the shortage of housing made life especially difficult for so many people. The great hopes for the future showed no sign of being achieved, and people were still asking when their troubles would end.

FURTHER READING

Blake, Lewis
Bromley in the Front Line
Revised Edition.
The Author, 1983.

Jones, Madeline
Finding out about Life in Britain in World War II.
Batsford, 1983.

Knowlden, Patricia
The Long Alert, 1937 - 1945.
Hollies Publishers, 1988.

Mack, Joanna and Humphries, Steve
The Making of Modern London 1939 - 1945: London at War.
Sidgwick and Jackson, 1985.

Pullen, Doris E.
Wartime memories: A Collection of Personal Memories of the Second World War.
Merlin Books, 1986.

Wallace, Graham.
R.A.F. Biggin Hill.
Tandem, 1969.

The Local Studies Library and Archives Section
at Bromley Central Library contains valuable materials for
project work and research.
Major files of local newspapers are also
available for consultation.

PICTURE INDEX

ABBREVIATIONS USED IN TEXT

ADC	Air Defence Command
ARP	Air Raid Precautions
ASS	Army Special Staff
CBE	Commander of the order of the British Empire
DFC	Distinguished Flying Cross
DFM	Distinguished Flying Medal
DSO	Distinguished Service Order
GCB	Knight of the Grand Cross order of the Bath
LDV	Local Defence Volunteer
MC	Military Cross
MVO	Marshallese Women's Organisation
WVS	Womens Voluntary Service
VC	Victoria Cross
VE	Victory in Europe
VJ	Victory in Japan

ACKNOWLEDGEMENTS

The author would like to thank the following people for their involvement with the book:

The staff at Bromley Central Library for their enthusiastic advice and support, particularly Pat Jones, Elizabeth Silverthorne, and Alex Freeman.

Mr Alan Goldsmith and Miss Frances Dawson for providing valuable recollections.

Indebtedness recorded to the authors of the following books "Bromley in the Front Line" by Lewis Blake, and "R.A.F. Biggin Hill" by Graham Wallace.

Patricia Knowlden, author of "The Long Alert 1937-1945" for uncovering the Richmal Crompton story, after the author had failed.

Mrs Gloria Richardson for information about Cudham Primary school.

PICTURE CREDITS

Air Displays International, Biggin Hill.

Black Horse Public House, Biggin Hill.

Bromley Central Library; Archives and Local Studies Department.

The Trustees of The Imperial War Museum, London.

Kentish Times Newspapers Limited.

R.A.F. Hendon.

Mr R. Spencer, London Borough Of Bromley.

John Topham Picture Library.